# Quilts for Babies & Kids

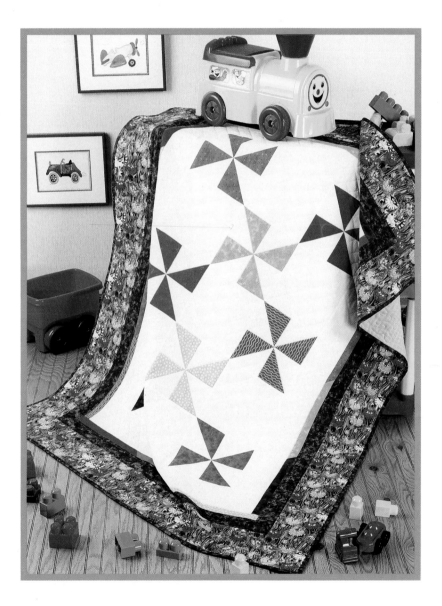

CREATED FOR LEISURE ARTS BY HOUSE OF WHITE BIRCHES

# Contents

**QUILTS FOR BABIES & KIDS** ©2003, 2001, 2000, 1999, 1998, 1997 House of White Birches, 306 East Parr Road, Berne, IN 46711, (260) 589-4000. Customer_Service@ whitebirches.com. Made in USA.

**ISBN: 1-57486-345-2**

**CREDITS:** Love Your Baby, page 41; Tropical Delight, page 46; Mini Sailboats, page 91, provided by Coats & Clark. Easter Baby Quilt, page 70, provided by DMC.

# Introduction

A peacefully sleeping child is a wondrous sight; especially when that child is wrapped in a quilt made by you with love. The child literally sleeps away the hours of your labor.

Chicks on Parade

Here you will find a collection of warm quilts to make for your favorite child. Whether it is a new quilt for a brand-new baby or a fun present for a delightful child, you are sure to find it in this collection.

Ruffles & Bows

If it's sweetness that you are looking for, try re-creating Ruffles & Bows on page 76. A few yards of fabric, some appliquéd hearts, a ruffle, a few delightful hours spent sewing, and you will have the perfect quilt to welcome a new baby.

Mouse to Tower

For the child who is attracted by whimsy, you'll want to make Chicks on Parade on page 15 or Mouse to Tower on page 63. They are certain to bring smiles to a happy child.

If you are looking for a traditional quilt in a new garb, follow the plans for Yo-Ho-Ho on page 21 and Thomas & Emma Mouse on page 32. Both of these quilts use the traditional Drunkard's Path quilt block in a new and innovative manner.

Thomas & Emma Mouse

Whatever your choice of quilt, remember that a childhood quilt leaves an indelible impression upon a child. Years later the sight of the quilt will surely bring back a host of memories of a loved one no longer here.

# Rainbow Sherbet

BY DAN & SUSAN SULLIVAN

Children love bright colors, and what baby wouldn't be pleased with this quilt. Combine many bright colored fabrics to create this delightful project. The quilt is easy to make because the pieces are simple 3" squares, but when it's put together, the quilt will garner bravos from young and old alike!

## Project Specifications
Quilt Size: 38½" x 48½"

## Fabric & Batting
- ⅛ yard each 2 yellow, 2 orange, 2 rose, 2 blue, 2 purple and 2 green prints
- ¼ yard green print
- ¼ yard black solid
- 1¼ yards rainbow solid
- Backing 42" x 52"
- Batting 42" x 52"
- 5¼ yards self-made or purchased binding

## Supplies & Tools
- All-purpose thread to match fabrics
- Basic sewing tools and supplies

## Instructions
1. Cut 3" x 3" squares from fabrics as directed in the Color Key/Cutting Chart.

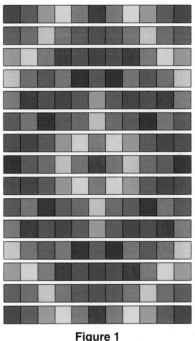

**Figure 1**
Arrange squares in rows as shown.

2. Referring to Color Key and Figure 1, arrange squares in rows. Join squares in rows; press. Join rows to complete pieced center; press.

3. Cut two strips black solid 2" x 38"; sew a strip to opposite long sides of pieced center. Press seams toward strips.

# Rainbow Sherbet

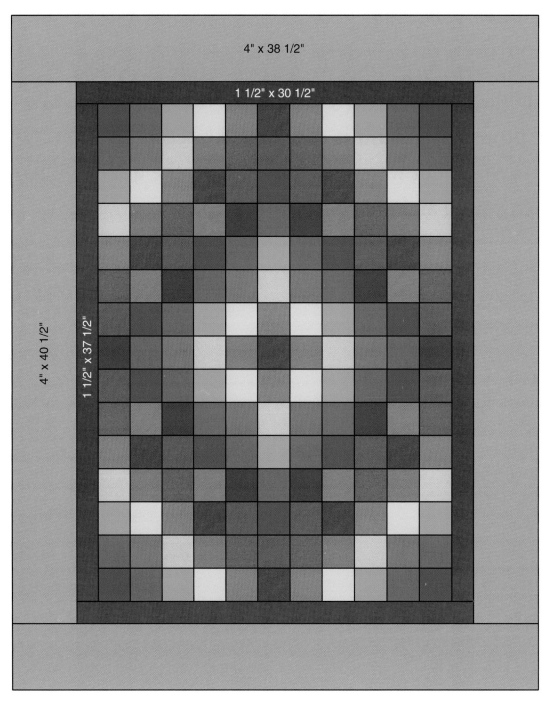

4" x 38 1/2"

1 1/2" x 30 1/2"

4" x 40 1/2"

1 1/2" x 37 1/2"

**Rainbow Sherbet**
Placement Diagram
38 1/2" x 48 1/2"

**COLOR KEY/CUTTING CHART**
- Green 1—cut 14
- Green 2—cut 24
- Green 3—cut 10
- Yellow 4—cut 12
- Yellow 5—cut 12
- Orange 6—cut 14
- Orange 7—cut 10
- Rose 8—cut 12
- Rose 9—cut 11
- Purple 10—cut 12
- Purple 10—cut 10
- Blue 12—cut 10
- Blue 13—cut 14

4. Cut two strips black solid 2" x 31"; sew to top and bottom of pieced center. Press seams toward strips.

5. Cut two strips rainbow solid 4½" x 41½" from fabric length; sew a strip to opposite long sides of pieced center. Press seams toward strips.

6. Cut two strips rainbow print 4½" x 39" from fabric length; sew to top and bottom of pieced center. Press seams toward strips.

7. Sandwich batting between completed top and prepared backing. Pin or baste layers together to hold flat.

8. Machine-quilt in the ditch of seams or as desired. When quilting is complete, remove pins or basting, trim threads and trim edges even.

9. Bind edges with self-made or purchased binding to finish. ❖

# Pinwheel Play

BY JULIE WEAVER

Eight easy-to-make pinwheels form the center of this quilt, but it is the chubby cat faces in the border print that add the excitement and turn this simple quilt into the focal point of a child's room. If your border print is a directional one, such as the cat print used in the photographed quilt, you will need to cut the border strips so that when stitched, the pieces show the print in an upright position. The top and bottom borders, therefore, must be cut from the fabric width while the side strips are cut from the length. This means more fabric is needed than if a nondirectional print is used.

# Pinwheel Play

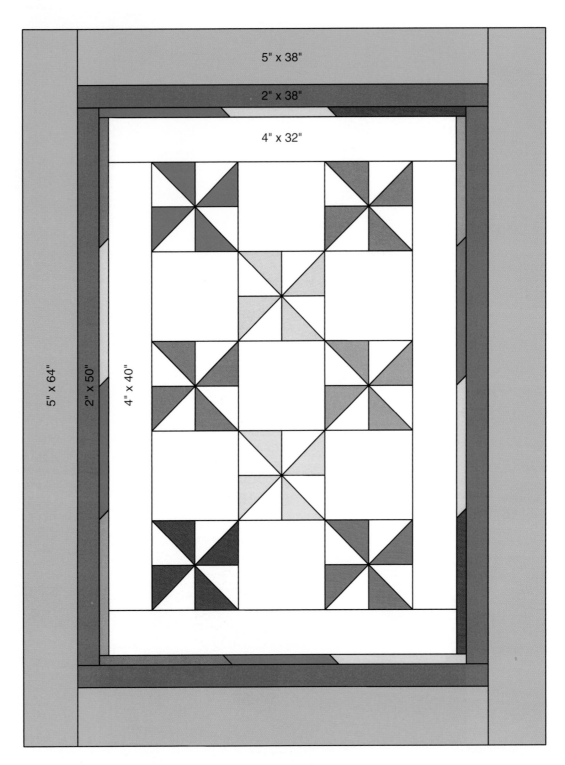

5" x 38"

2" x 38"

4" x 32"

5" x 64"

2" x 50"

4" x 40"

**Pinwheel Play**
Placement Diagram
48" x 64"

# Pinwheel Play

## Project Specifications

Quilt Size: 48" x 64"
Block Size: 8" x 8"
Number of Blocks: 8 pieced; 7 solid

## Fabric & Batting

- 2 fat quarters of each color family in prints, solids or mottled: red, yellow, blue and orange
- ½ yard dark green mottled
- 1½ yards white-on-white print
- 2¼ yards directional cat print or 1 yard non-directional print
- Backing 52" x 68"
- Batting 52" x 68"
- 6½ yards self-made or purchased binding

## Supplies & Tools

- Neutral color all-purpose thread
- Green and white quilting thread
- Basic sewing tools and supplies, rotary cutter, mat and ruler

## Instructions

1. Cut two 4⅞" x 4⅞" squares from each of the fabric fat quarters.

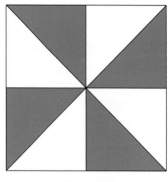

**Pinwheel**
8" x 8" Block

2. Cut two strips white-on-white print 4⅞" by fabric width; subcut into sixteen 4⅞" square segments.

3. Layer a white-on-white print square with a colored square with right sides together; draw a diagonal line across the lighter of the layered squares.

4. Sew ¼" on each side of the drawn line as shown in Figure 1.

5. Cut on the drawn line between the stitching line as shown in Figure 2. Open the two resulting stitched units; press with seam toward darkest fabric. Repeat for 32 units.

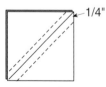

**Figure 1**
Sew 1/4" on each
side of the drawn line.

**Figure 2**
Cut on the drawn line
between the stitching
lines as shown.

# Pinwheel Play

6. Arrange four same-colored pieces as shown in Figure 3; join to complete one block. Repeat for eight blocks.

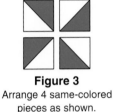

**Figure 3**
Arrange 4 same-colored
pieces as shown.

7. Cut two strips white-on-white print 8½" by fabric width; subcut strips into 8½" square units to make background squares. You will need seven background squares.

8. Join two Pinwheel blocks with one background square to make a row; press seams toward blocks. Repeat for three rows.

9. Join two background squares with one Pinwheel block to make a row; press seams toward block. Repeat for two rows.

10. Join the rows referring to the Placement Diagram; press seams in one direction.

11. Cut two strips each 4½" x 32½" and 4½" x 40½" white-on-white print. Sew the longer strips to opposite long sides and shorter strips to the top and bottom; press seams toward strips.

12. Cut two strips from each fat quarter 1½" by fabric width. Subcut each strip into one 13" and one 12¼" piece.

13. Join four different color 13" pieces with a diagonal seam as shown in Figure 4; repeat for two strips to create side border strips. Sew a strip to opposite long sides; press seams toward strips and trim excess.

14. Join four different color 12¼" pieces with a diagonal seam, again referring to Figure 4; repeat for two strips. Sew a strip to the top and bottom; press seams toward strips and trim excess.

**Figure 4**
Join 4 different color 13"
pieces with a diagonal seam.

15. Cut and piece two strips each dark green mottled 2½" x 38½" and 2½" x 50½". Sew the longer strips to opposite long sides and shorter strips to the top and bottom of the pieced center; press seams toward strips.

16. Cut two strips 5½" x 38½" across width of directional print; sew to the top and bottom of the pieced center. Press seams toward strips.

17. Cut two strips 5½" x 64½" along length of directional print; sew a strip to opposite long sides of the pieced center. Press seams toward strips.

18. Sandwich batting between completed top and prepared backing piece; pin or baste layers together to hold flat.

19. Quilt as desired by hand or machine.
*Note: The quilt shown was machine-quilted in* *the background areas with white quilting thread in a crosshatch design. The border strips were quilted in the ditch and ¼" from seams using green quilting thread.*

20. When quilting is complete, trim edges even; remove pins or basting.

21. Bind edges with self-made or purchased binding to finish. ❖

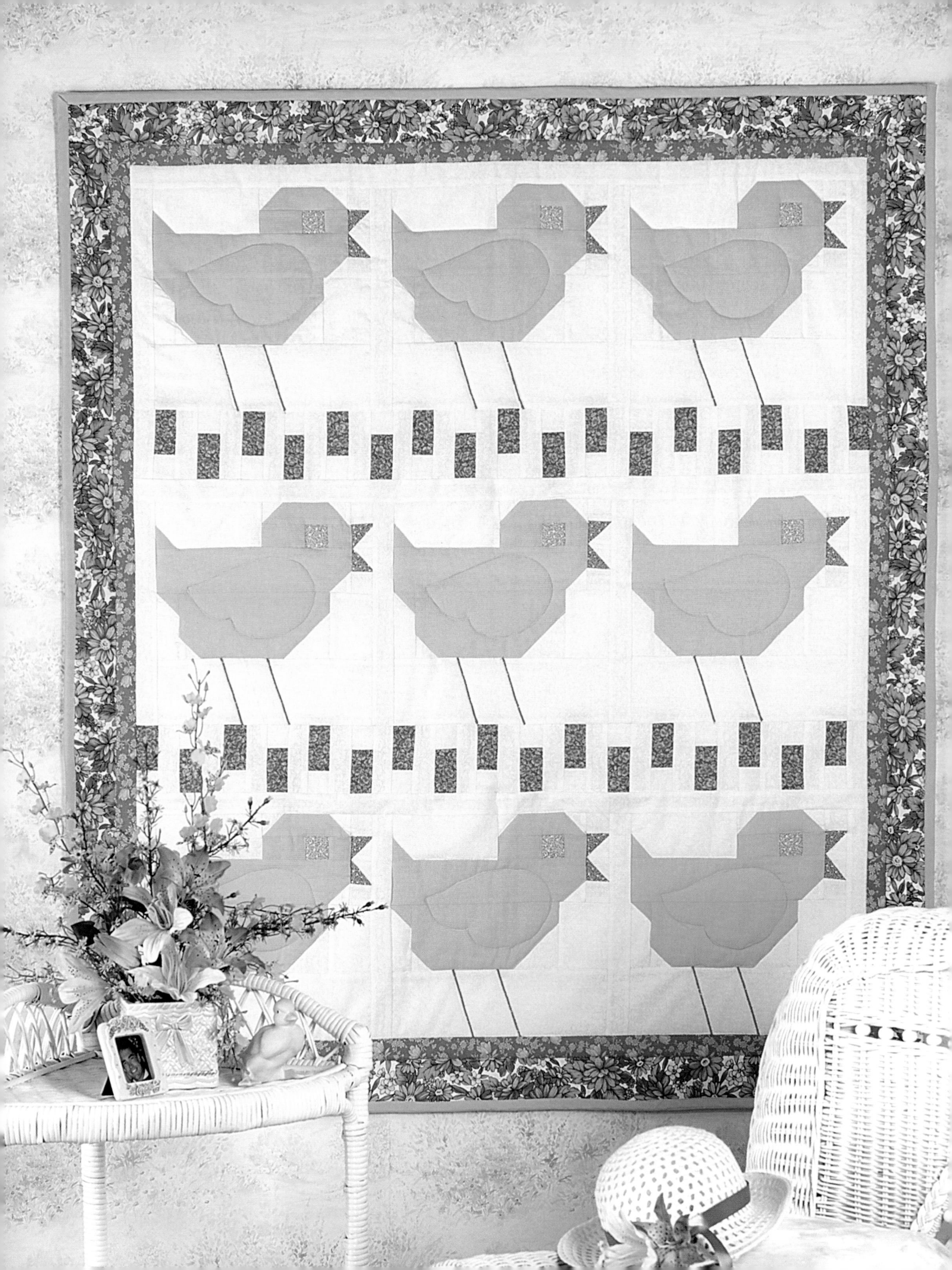

# Chicks on Parade

BY CHERYL FALL

Nine baby chicks parade across this adorable quilt right into the hearts of all who see them. At first glance, the chicks look as if they have been appliquéd onto the quilt top, but they are actually pieced—a real bonus for those quilters who prefer piecing to appliqué.

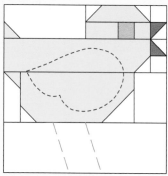

**Chicks**
10" x 10" Block

## Project Specifications

Quilt Size: 40" x 45"

Block Size: 10" x 10"

## Fabric & Batting

- 1½ yards off-white tone-on-tone print
- 1 yard yellow solid
- ¾ yard rose print
- ½ yard floral print
- ½ yard green print
- 1 square orange print 8" x 8"
- 1 square pink print 8" x 8"
- Backing 44" x 50"
- Batting 44" x 50"

## Supplies & Tools

- Matching color all-purpose thread
- 1 spool tango rayon machine embroidery thread
- 1 spool monofilament thread
- 2 packages extra-wide, double-fold bias tape
- Basic sewing supplies and tools, small rotary cutter, mat and ruler

## Instructions

*Note: All seam allowances are ¼" and are included in all measurements given.*

1. Cut the following strips in the order given: rose print—two strips each 1½" x 41½" and 1½" x 34½"; and floral print—two strips each 2½" x 41½" and 2½" x 40½".

2. Cut the following (refer to *Note following cutting instructions): A—nine off-white strips 2½" x 5½"; B*—nine yellow squares 1⅞" x 1⅞"; C*—18 off-white squares 1⅞" x 1⅞"; D—nine yellow pieces 1½" x 2½"; E—nine squares each pink and yellow and 18 squares off-white 1½" x 1½"; F—nine pieces yellow 1½" x 4½"; G—nine pieces yellow 2½" x 9½"; H—nine pieces yellow 3½" x 7½"; I*—five squares off-white 2⅞" x 2⅞; J—nine pieces off-white 2½" x 3½"; K—nine strips off-white 3½" x 10½"; and L—nine pieces off-white 1½" x 3½".

# Chicks on Parade

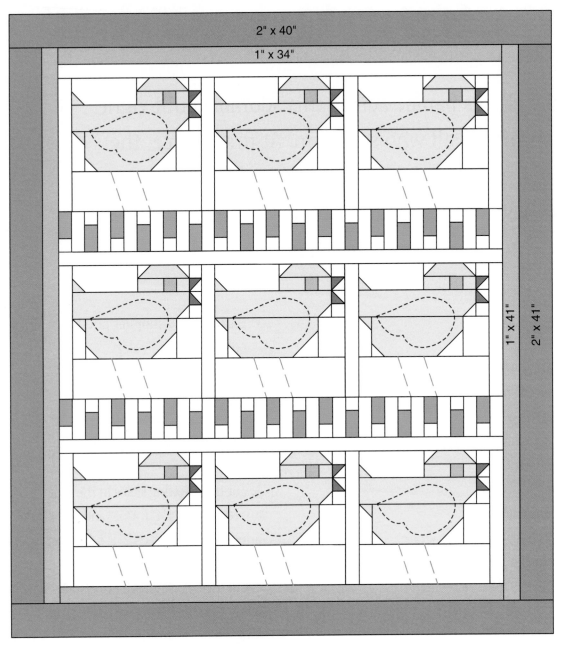

2" x 40"

1" x 34"

1" x 41"

2" x 41"

**Chicks on Parade**
Placement Diagram
40" x 45"

*Note: Cut each of the squares for B, C and I in half on the diagonal to make two triangles from each square. You will have 18 for B, 36 for C and 10 for I. Discard one of the I triangles.*

3. Cut one square each 8" x 8" from orange and off-white fabrics. Mark nine 1⅞" x 1⅞" squares in three rows on the wrong side of the off-white square. Mark a diagonal line through each square as shown in Figure 1.

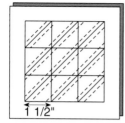

**Figure 1**
Draw nine 1 7/8" squares on the wrong side of the 8" x 8" square of off-white. Draw a diagonal line through each square. Layer with orange square; stitch 1/4" from diagonal line.

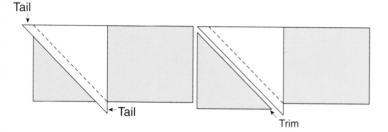

When attaching triangle pieces to square-edge pieces, leave the tails of the triangles extending 1/4" from the edges as shown. Trim away the excess from the square-edge piece even with the bias edges of the triangle to eliminate bulk.

**4.** Pin the orange and off-white squares rights sides together; stitch ¼" on each side of the diagonal lines as shown in Figure 1.

**5.** Cut squares apart; cut each square in half along the diagonal line. Press triangles open to make a square for the beak sections (marked BS on drawings).

**6.** Referring to Figures 2 assemble Row 1; repeat for Rows 2 and 3 referring to Figures 3 and 4. Press after each addition.

**7.** Mark the leg lines on the K pieces for Row 4 referring to Figure 5. Machine-embroider the legs

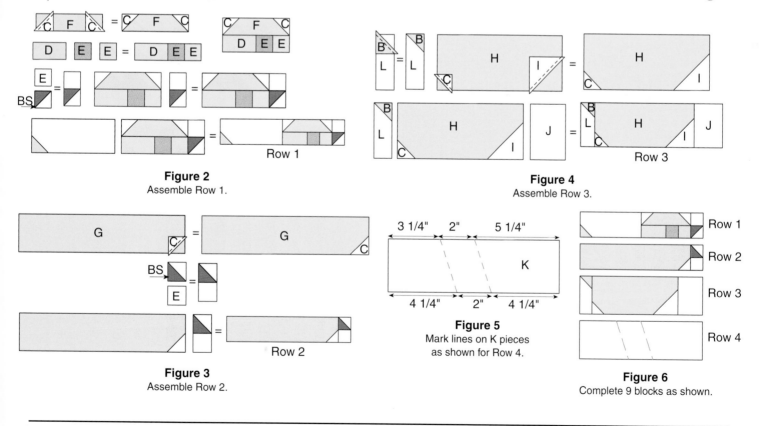

**Figure 2**
Assemble Row 1.

**Figure 3**
Assemble Row 2.

**Figure 4**
Assemble Row 3.

**Figure 5**
Mark lines on K pieces as shown for Row 4.

**Figure 6**
Complete 9 blocks as shown.

# Chicks on Parade

using rayon thread and a medium-width machine satin stitch.

8. Stitch Rows 1 through 4 together to make nine complete blocks as shown in Figure 6; press.

9. To make the grass strip, cut two strips green 2½" by fabric width and two strips off-white 1½" by fabric width. Sew a green strip to an off-white strip; repeat. Press seam allowances toward green strip.

10. Cut strips into 1½" segments; you will need 34 segments. Cut two strips off-white 3½" by fabric width. Cut 34 segments 1½" wide.

11. Sew 17 green/off-white 1½" segments together with 17 off-white 1½" segments referring to Figure 7 for placement to make one leaf strip; repeat for two strips; press.

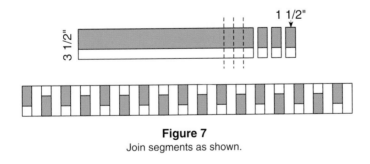

**Figure 7**
Join segments as shown.

12. Cut 12 M strips 1½" x 10½" from off-white.

Sew four strips alternately with three blocks to make a block row as shown in Figure 8; repeat for three block rows. Cut three N strips 1½" x 34½" from off-white. Sew to the top of the three block rows as shown in Figure 9.

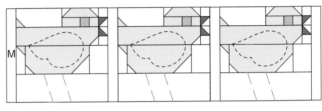

**Figure 8**
Join blocks with M strips.

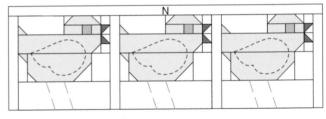

**Figure 9**
Sew N strips to top of each block row.

13. Referring to Figure 10, join the three block rows with two grass rows to make the quilt center; press.

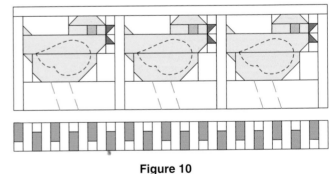

**Figure 10**
Join block rows with grass rows.

14. Sew the rose print 1½" x 34½" sashing strip cut in step 1 to the top and bottom; press. Sew the 1½" x 41½" strips to opposite sides; press. Sew the 2½" x 41½" floral print strips cut in step 1 to sides; sew 2½" x 40½" strips to top and bottom. Press.

15. Transfer the wing quilting design to the pieced chicks referring to the Placement Diagram.

16. Sandwich the batting between the completed top and prepared backing piece. Baste or pin the layers together to hold flat.

17. Machine-quilt along the seam lines and marked wing lines with the clear nylon monofilament thread in the top of the machine and all-purpose thread in the bobbin. Stitch close to the raw edges of the top; trim away excess batting and backing.

18. Bind edges of quilt with bias tape. ❖

**Wing Quilting Design**

# Yo-Ho-Ho

BY KAREN NEARY

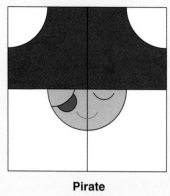

**Pirate**
12" x 12" Block

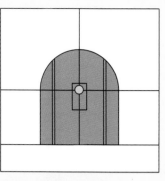

**Treasure Chest**
12" x 12" Block

Dig into your treasure chest for fabrics to make this unique and innovative pirate quilt! Look closely, and you'll recognize that the templates normally used to make a Drunkard's Path quilt are used here to create both the pirate and the treasure chest blocks. So, "yo, ho, ho," let's make a quilt that's fun!

## Project Specifications

Quilt Size: 56" x 84"

Block Size: 12" x 12"

Number of Blocks: 12

## Fabric & Batting

- ⅞ yard pink solid
- ½ yard black solid
- 1¼ yards white print
- 2 yards blue solid
- 2¼ yards gold solid
- Backing 60" x 88"
- 8 yards self-made or purchased binding

## Supplies & Tools

- Neutral color all-purpose thread
- Black, pink and brown machine-embroidery thread
- ½ yard tear-off fabric stabilizer

- 5 dozen gold sequins
- 6 (½") gold buttons
- Drunkard's Path templates for 6" finished block or template material
- Basic sewing tools and supplies

## Instructions

1. Using purchased templates or using pattern pieces given to prepare templates, cut 12 white print A pieces and 12 black solid B pieces for Pirate blocks.

2. Sew A to B; repeat for 12 A-B units. Press seams toward A.

3. Cut 12 pink solid A pieces and 12 white print B pieces. Sew A to B; repeat for 12 A-B units.

4. Sew two white/black A-B units to two pink/white

# Yo-Ho-Ho

**Yo-Ho-Ho**
Placement Diagram
56" x 84"

A-B units to complete one Pirate block as shown in Figure 1; repeat for six blocks; press.

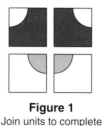

**Figure 1**
Join units to complete
1 Pirate block

5. Transfer marks for eyes and patches to pink A pieces using marks on patterns given as a guide for placement.

6. Place a piece of fabric stabilizer behind each piece. Using black thread, machine-embroider eyes; machine-embroider mouth with pink thread. For two blocks use an eye patch; cut patch sections from blue solid and place randomly or referring to the Placement Diagram and photo. Machine-appliqué in place using black thread referring to lines on pattern for placement.

7. Cut 12 gold solid A pieces and 12 white print B pieces; sew A to B. Press seams toward A; repeat for 12 units for tops of Treasure Chest blocks. Join two units as shown in Figure 2; repeat for six units.

8. For each bottom section, cut one piece each gold solid and white print 3½" x 4½". Sew together on 4½" sides referring to Figure 3. Repeat for 12 units. Sew two white/gold units together on gold edges again referring to Figure 3; repeat for 6 units and press.

**Figure 2**
Join 2 units as shown.

**Figure 3**
Sew together on
4 1/2" sides.

9. Cut six rectangles white print 2½" x 12½". Sew one of these rectangles to the bottom of each unit pieced in step 8 to complete bottom section; press.

10. Join one bottom section and one A-B unit pieced in step 7 to complete one Treasure Chest block as shown in Figure 4.

**Figure 4**
Join 2 pieced sections to complete
1 Treasure Chest block.

11. Mark a vertical line 1" from each side of treasure chest as shown in Figure 5. Place a piece of fabric stabilizer behind treasure chest section. Machine-stitch along the marked line with brown thread. Stitch again ⅛" from first line. Mark a 1" x 1½" rectangle in the center of the chest again referring to Figure 5; stitch to make lock. Repeat for all Treasure Chest blocks.

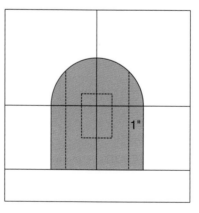

**Figure 5**
Mark vertical line 1" from each side
of treasure chest; mark 1" x 1 1/2"
rectangle in center.

# Yo-Ho-Ho

12. Cut eight strips blue solid 2" x 12½". Referring to Placement Diagram, join three blocks with two strips to make a block row; repeat for four blocks rows. Press seams toward strips.

13. Cut five strips blue solid 2" x 39½". Join block rows with strips, beginning and ending with a strip, to complete pieced center; press seams toward strips.

14. Cut and piece two strips blue solid 2" x 56"; sew to opposite long sides of quilt center. Press seams toward strips.

15. Cut two strips gold solid 2¾" x 42½"; sew to top and bottom of pieced center. Press seams toward strips. Cut two strips gold print 3½" x 60½"; sew to opposite long sides of pieced center. Press seams toward gold strips.

16. Cut 57 squares each gold and blue solids 4⅞" x 4⅞". Cut each square in half on one diagonal to make 114 triangles of each color.

17. Sew a blue triangle to a gold triangle; repeat for 114 units.

18. Join 14 triangles to make a strip as shown in Figure 6; press seams in one direction. Repeat for six rows. Join four rows as shown in Figure 7; sew

to top of pieced center referring to the Placement Diagram. Press seams toward strips.

**Figure 6**
Join 14 triangles to make a strip.

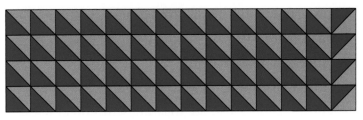

**Figure 7**
Join 4 rows for top as shown.

19. Join two rows; sew to bottom of pieced center, referring to the Placement Diagram.

20. Join 15 units for side strips referring to the Placement Diagram for positioning of triangle/ squares. Repeat for two strips. Sew a strip to each long side; press seams toward strips.

21. Sandwich fleece between pieced top and prepared backing; pin or baste layers to hold flat.

22. Quilt as desired by hand or machine. When quilting is complete, trim edge even. Bind with self-made or purchased binding.

23. Sew a gold button to the center of each treasure

chest lock. Hand-stitch sequins around bottom of
treasure chest to look like gold doubloons to finish. ❖

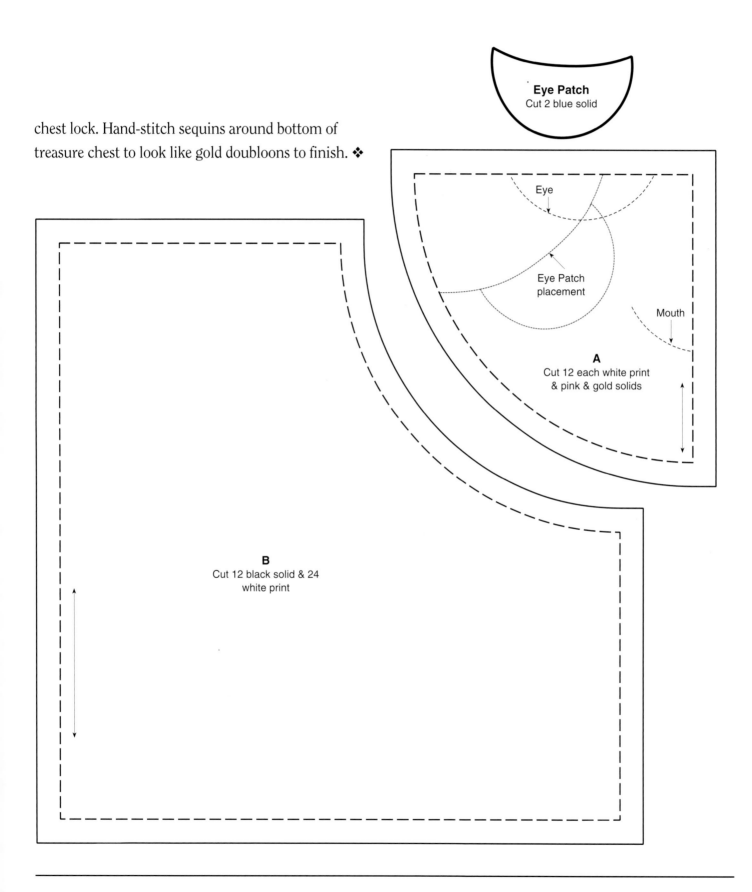

**Eye Patch**
Cut 2 blue solid

Eye

Eye Patch
placement

Mouth

**A**
Cut 12 each white print
& pink & gold solids

**B**
Cut 12 black solid & 24
white print

# Circus Tricks

BY SUE HARVEY

If you've ever purchased a wonderful circus print fabric and then were dismayed at cutting it up, this is the quilt for you. The Hugs and Kisses blocks, which form the center of this quilt, are the perfect spots for large sections of that circus print. While this quilt is made with a predominantly pink and blue print, you may prefer another color scheme for your quilt. No matter what the colors, this quilt is sure to please any child.

# Circus Tricks

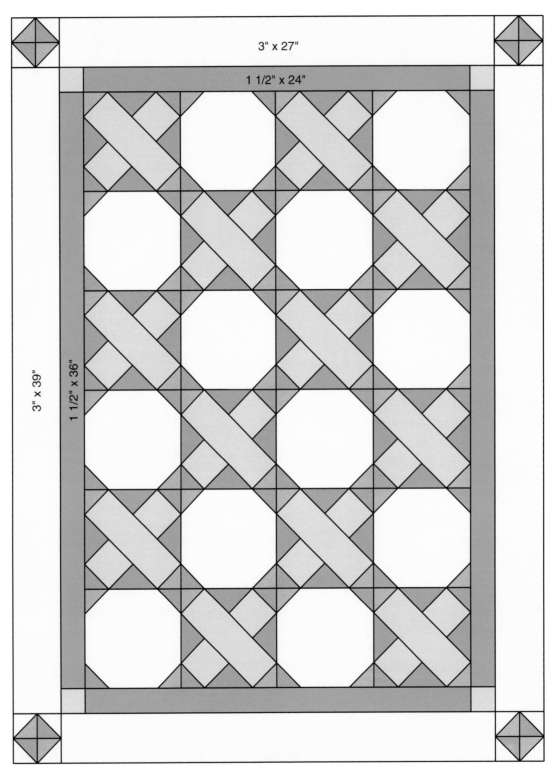

3" x 27"

1 1/2" x 24"

3" x 39"

1 1/2" x 36"

**Circus Tricks**
Placement Diagram
33" x 45"

# Circus Tricks

## Project Specifications

Quilt Size: 33" x 45"

Block Size: 12" x 12"

Number of Blocks: 6

## Fabric & Batting

- ½ yard multicolored dot
- ½ yard each pink and blue solids
- ¾ yard green solid
- 1 yard circus print
- Backing 37" x 49"
- Batting 37" x 49"

## Supplies & Tools

- All-purpose thread to match fabrics
- Off-white machine-quilting thread
- Basic sewing tools and supplies, rotary cutter, mat and ruler

## Instructions

1. Cut two strips 6½" by fabric width circus print; cut each strip into 6½" square segments for A. You will need 12 A squares.

2. Cut two strips each pink and blue solids 2" by fabric width; cut each strip into 2" square segments for B. You will need 24 B squares of each color.

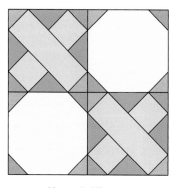

**Hugs & Kisses**
12" x 12" Block

3. Cut one strip each pink and blue solids and circus print 2⅜" by fabric width; subcut each strip into 2⅜" square segments. Cut each square on one diagonal to make F triangles. You will need 16 circus print and 32 each pink solid and blue solid F triangles.

4. Cut two strips 2⅝" by fabric width multicolored dot; cut each strip into 2⅝" square segments for C. You will need 24 C squares.

5. Cut one strip 6⅞" by fabric width multicolored dot; cut into 2⅝" segments for E. You will need 12 E rectangles.

6. Cut two strips 4¼" by fabric width green solid; subcut each strip into 4¼" square segments. Cut each square on both diagonals to make D triangles. You will need 48 D triangles.

7. Draw a diagonal line on the wrong side of each B square.

8. Place a pink B square right sides together on opposite corners of A as shown in Figure 1. Stitch on the marked lines; trim seam allowance to ¼" and press B triangles open as shown in Figure 2. Repeat with blue B squares on the remaining corners of A to make an O unit as shown in Figure 3. Repeat for 12 O units.

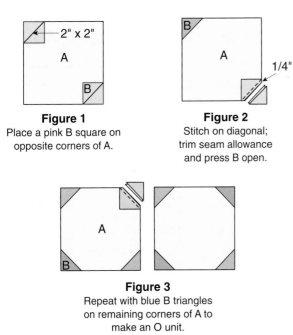

**Figure 1**
Place a pink B square on opposite corners of A.

**Figure 2**
Stitch on diagonal; trim seam allowance and press B open.

**Figure 3**
Repeat with blue B triangles on remaining corners of A to make an O unit.

9. Sew D to opposite sides of C; add a blue F triangle as shown in Figure 4. Repeat for two C-D-F units.

10. Sew a C-D-F unit to opposite long sides of E; add a pink F triangle to each remaining corner to make an X unit as shown in Figure 5. Repeat for 12 X units.

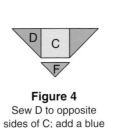
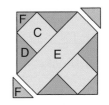

**Figure 4**
Sew D to opposite sides of C; add a blue F triangle.

**Figure 5**
Sew a C-D-F unit to opposite sides of E; add pink F triangles to make an X unit.

11. Sew an X unit to an O unit; repeat. Join the two X-O units to complete one Hugs and Kisses block; repeat for six blocks.

12. Join two blocks to make a block row referring to the Placement Diagram for positioning of blocks; repeat for three block rows.

13. Join the block rows to complete the pieced center.

14. Cut two strips each 2" x 24½" and 2" x 36½" green solid. Sew the longer strips to opposite long sides of the pieced center.

15. Cut four squares multicolored dot 2" x 2". Sew a square to each end of the remaining green solid strips. Sew a strip to remaining sides of the pieced center.

**16.** Cut two strips each 3½" x 27½" and 3½" x 39½" circus print. Sew the longer strips to opposite long sides of the pieced center.

**17.** Sew a circus print F to a pink solid F along the diagonal edge to make a pink F unit as shown in Figure 6; repeat for two pink F units and two blue F units. Join the F units to make a corner square as shown in Figure 7.

Make 2    Make 2

**Figure 6**
Make F units as shown.

**Figure 7**
Join F units to make a corner square.

**18.** Repeat step 17 to make four corner squares. Sew a corner square to each end of the remaining circus print strips. Sew a strip to remaining sides of the pieced center to complete the pieced top.

**19.** Sandwich batting between completed top and prepared backing piece; pin or baste to hold.

**20.** Hand- or machine-quilt as desired. *Note: The sample shown was machine-quilted in an allover meandering pattern. Remove pins or basting; trim edges with top.*

**21.** Cut two strips each pink, blue and green solids 3" by fabric width. Join strips along length to make a strip set staggering each strip 1" as shown in Figure 8.

1"

**Figure 8**
Join strips to make a strip set.

**22.** Trim one end of strip set at a 45-degree angle as shown in Figure 9. Cut into 2¼" strips, again referring to Figure 9.

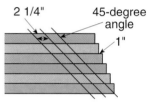

2 1/4"    45-degree angle

1"

**Figure 9**
Trim 1 end of strip set at a 45-degree angle; cut into 2 1/4" strips.

**23.** Join strips on short ends to make 5 yards bias binding as shown in Figure 10.

**Figure 10**
Join strips on short ends.

**24.** Fold binding strip in half along length with wrong sides together; press. Bind edges of quilt to finish. ❖

# Thomas & Emma Mouse

BY KAREN NEARY

If you thought that a Drunkard's Path template could only be used to create a Drunkard's Path quilt block, here is a creative block to prove you wrong. The templates that would normally make a Drunkard's Path patchwork block are used here as guides to cut the shirtfronts for both the little girl and little boy mouse. The little boy mouse wears a tuxedo while his partner is dressed in ribbons and lace. What could be cuter!

# Thomas & Emma Mouse

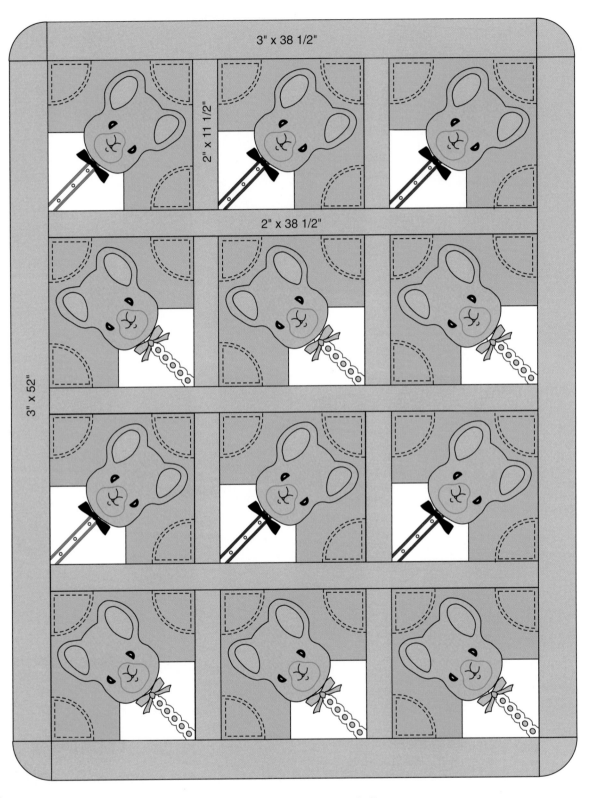

**Thomas & Emma Mouse Quilt**
Placement Diagram
44 1/2" x 58"

# Thomas & Emma Mouse

## Project Specifications

Quilt Size: 44½" x 58"
Block Size: 11½" x 11½"
Number of Blocks: 12

## Fabric & Batting

- 1½ yards blue print
- 3½ yards pink pin dot
- ½ yard gray solid
- 1¾ yards white solid
- Scraps pink solid for ears
- Backing 49" x 62"
- Quilter's fleece 49" x 62"
- 6 yards self-made or purchased binding

## Supplies & Tools

- Template material or Drunkard's Path 6" quilting templates
- All-purpose thread to match fabrics
- 1 spool black topstitching thread
- 1 spool each black, pink, white and gray machine-embroidery thread
- Small amount of fiberfill
- 18 (⅜") white buttons
- 1 yard white lace beading
- 1 yard ⅜"-wide black velvet ribbon
- 2 yards ⅜"-wide pink satin ribbon

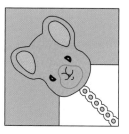 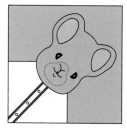

**Emma Mouse**
11 1/2" x 11 1/2" Block

**Thomas Mouse**
11 1/2" x 11 1/2" Block

- ½ yard medium weight fusible interfacing
- ½ yard tear-off fabric stabilizer
- 7 yards self-made or purchased binding
- Basic sewing tools and supplies

## Instructions

*Note: All seam allowances are ¼" and are included in the given measurements. The appliqué pieces do not require seam allowance.*

1. Cut 12 squares 12" x 12" blue print.

2. To make tuxedo shirt fronts, cut two strips white solid 11" by fabric width. Press each strip in half along length to mark center.

3. Beginning ¼" past center crease, make three rows of pin tucks on each side of the crease on each strip.

4. Position shirt front template on fabric so pin tucks are centered; cut six. Cut six shirt fronts from unstitched white solid for lining. Sew these together in pairs along shoulder seams only, right sides facing.

# Thomas & Emma Mouse

5. Turn, press; baste raw edges together and set aside.

6. Cut 12 shirt fronts from white solid. Insert pink ribbon in lace beading; cut lace into 6" lengths. Fold six shirt fronts in half and crease to mark center; topstitch lace along the center line. Sew together with linings as in step 3.

7. Position shirt fronts on blue squares with point of front in a corner. Topstitch in place along shoulder seams and neck edge. Baste together along remaining edges.

8. Cut mouse heads, snouts and ears as directed on pattern pieces. Transfer markings on head and snout to cut-out pieces.

9. Place a piece of tear-off stabilizer under each snout piece. With black topstitching thread in the top of the machine and all-purpose thread in the bobbin, straight-stitch along nose and mouth markings on snout pieces. Use pink to embroider tip of nose. Tie thread ends and carefully remove stabilizer.

10. Position snout on face; satin stitch in place using narrow width stitch and gray thread. With stabilizer underneath, machine embroider eyes with black and white threads and ears with pink thread; remove stabilizer.

11. Carefully clip an X in back of snout, stuff lightly and slipstitch back together with a few hand stitches.

12. With right side of mouse facing fusible side of interfacing, stitch completely around outside edge. Cut an X in center of interfacing, carefully turn mouse right side out. Clip curves, trim seams.

13. Position on block, overlapping neck edge of shirt by ¼". Press in place, being careful not to press stuffed snout. Repeat for remaining mice. *Note: Mice may be hand-appliquéd or topstitched in place around outside edges with matching thread.*

14. Cut eight pieces 2½" x 12" pink pin dot. Join three blocks with two strips to make rows, alternating rows of girl and boy mice as shown in Figure 1. Repeat for four rows; press seams toward strips.

15. Cut three strips pink pin dot 2½" x 39"; join rows with strips. Press seams toward strips.

16. Cut two strips 3½" x 52½" and two pieces 3½" x 39" pink pin dot. Cut four corner blocks pink pin dot. Sew the shorter strips to the top and bottom. Sew a corner block to each end of the longer strips; sew to opposite sides. Press seams toward strips.

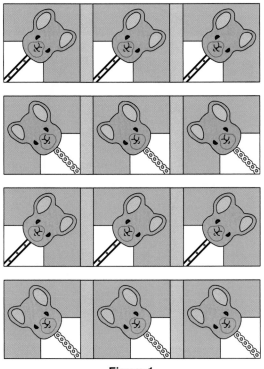

**Figure 1**
Join blocks to make rows alternating
boy and girl blocks as shown.

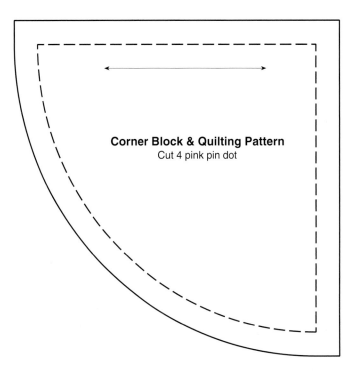

**Corner Block & Quilting Pattern**
Cut 4 pink pin dot

17. Sandwich batting between the completed top and prepared backing piece. Pin or baste layers together to hold flat.

18. Quilt as desired by hand or machine. When quilting is complete, trim edges even. Bind with self-made or purchased binding.

19. Cut six 6" lengths black velvet and pink satin ribbon. Tie a bow from each piece. Tack pink bows to girl heads and black bows to boy necks to finish. ❖

# Thomas & Emma Mouse

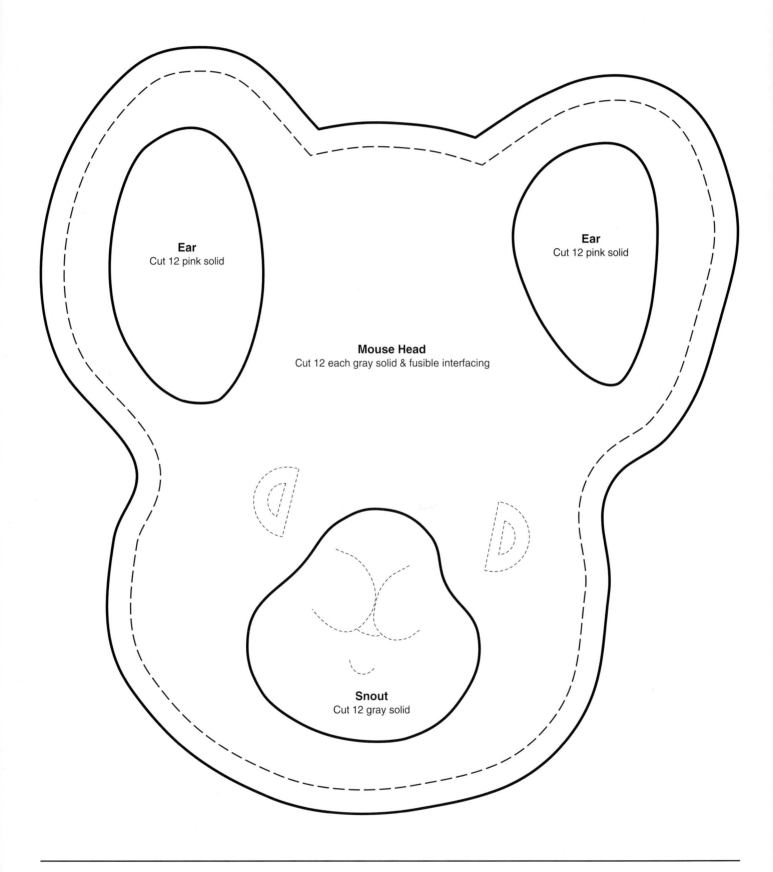

**Ear**
Cut 12 pink solid

**Ear**
Cut 12 pink solid

**Mouse Head**
Cut 12 each gray solid & fusible interfacing

**Snout**
Cut 12 gray solid

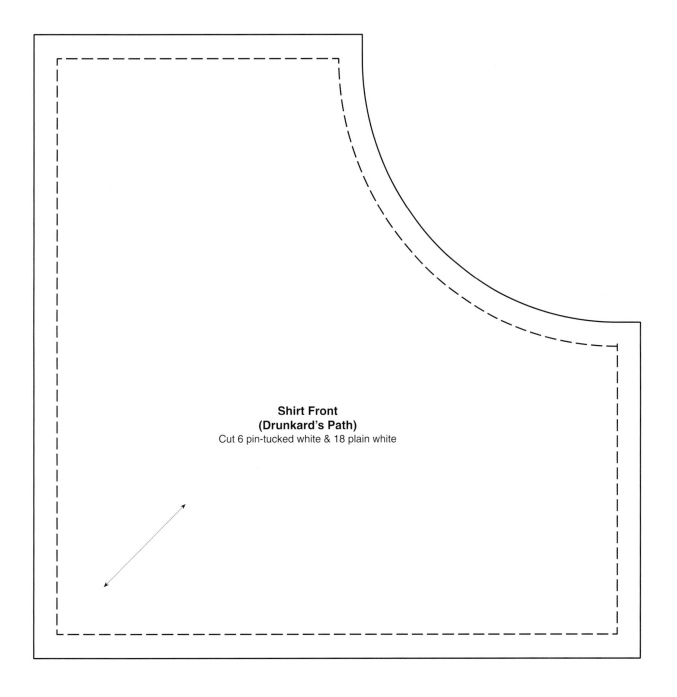

**Shirt Front
(Drunkard's Path)**
Cut 6 pin-tucked white & 18 plain white

# Love Your Baby

BY MICHELE CRAWFORD

Two blocks—House Jack Built and Pinwheel—combine to create this vibrant baby quilt. The red hearts in the center of the Jack blocks will certainly broadcast your love for that special baby.

**House Jack Built**
10" x 10" Block

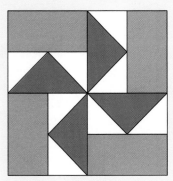

**Pinwheel**
10" x 10" Block

## Project Specifications

Quilt Size: 41" x 51½"
Block Size: 10" x 10"
Number of Blocks: 12

## Fabric & Batting

- ⅓ yard yellow solid
- ½ yard yellow dot
- ½ yard blue print
- ½ yard red print
- ⅝ yard animal print
- ¾ yard white print
- Backing 45" x 56"
- 1⅝ yards quilter's fleece

## Supplies & Tools

- White, pilot blue, atom red and spark gold all-purpose thread
- Hot pumpkin rayon color twist thread
- White and red hand-quilting thread
- Clear nylon monofilament
- 2 packages atom red wide bias tape
- ⅛ yard fusible transfer web
- Basic sewing tools and supplies

## Instructions

### Making House Jack Built Blocks

1. To make House Jack Built blocks, cut the following from white print: six squares 4" x 4" for A; one strip 3⅜" by fabric width and cut into twelve 3⅜" square segments—cut each segment in half on one diagonal to make 24 B triangles; and two strips 4⅜" by fabric width and cut into twelve 4⅜" square segments—cut each segment in half on one diagonal to make 24 C triangles.

# Love Your Baby

4 1/2" x 4 1/2"

1/2" x 31"    1/2" x 1/2"

1/2" x 41 1/2"

4 1/2" x 42 1/2"

**Love Your Baby Quilt**
Placement Diagram
41" x 51 1/2"

2. Cut one strip each blue print, yellow dot and red print 4" by fabric width; cut each strip into twenty-four 1¾" segments for D rectangles.

3. To piece one House Jack Built block, join one D rectangle of each fabric referring to Figure 1 for color placement; trim to 4" x 4". Repeat for four units.

4. Sew a B triangle to the red print side of each D unit and two C triangles to two opposite sides of two D units as shown in Figure 2.

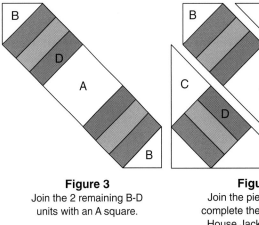

**Figure 3**
Join the 2 remaining B-D units with an A square.

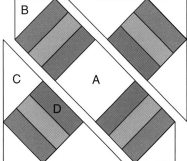

**Figure 4**
Join the pieced units to complete the piecing for 1 House Jack Built block.

**Figure 1**
Join 1 D rectangle of each fabric to make a square.

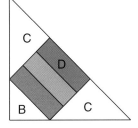

**Figure 2**
Sew a B triangle to the red print side of each D unit and 2 C triangles to 2 opposite sides of 2 D unites

5. Join the two remaining B-D units with an A square as shown in Figure 3. Join the pieced units to complete the piecing for one House Jack Built block as shown in Figure 4; press. Repeat for six blocks.

6. Prepare template for heart shape. Trace heart shape on the paper side of the fusible transfer web as directed on pattern for number to cut. Cut out shapes, leaving a margin around each shape.

7. Cut a 3" x 17" strip red print. Fuse the heart shapes to the wrong side of the red print strip. Cut out heart shapes on traced lines; remove paper backing.

8. Center and fuse a heart shape in each A square of each pieced block; set aside.

## Making Pinwheel Blocks

1. To make Pinwheel blocks, cut two strips white print 3⅜" by fabric width; cut strips into 3⅜" square segments. You will need 24 segments. Cut each square segment in half on one diagonal to make 48 E triangles.

2. Cut two strips blue print 4⅜" by fabric width; cut strips into 4⅜" square segments. You will need 12 segments. Cut each segment in half on one diagonal to make 24 F triangles.

# Love Your Baby

3. Cut two strips yellow dot 5½" by fabric width; cut strips into twenty-four 3" segments for G.

4. To piece one Pinwheel block, sew an E triangle to each short side of F as shown in Figure 5; repeat for four E-F units. Sew G to each unit as shown in Figure 6. Join the four E-F-G units to complete one block as shown in Figure 7; press. Repeat for six blocks.

**Figure 5**
Sew an E triangle to each short side of F.

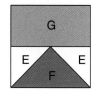

**Figure 6**
Sew G to each unit.

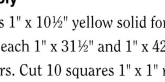

**Figure 7**
Join the 4 E-F-G units to complete 1 block.

## Quilt Assembly

1. Cut 17 strips 1" x 10½" yellow solid for sashing and two strips each 1" x 31½" and 1" x 42" yellow solid for borders. Cut 10 squares 1" x 1" red print for sashing squares.

2. Join two 1" x 10½" strips yellow solid with two 1" x 1" red print squares to make a sashing row as shown in Figure 8; repeat for three sashing rows.

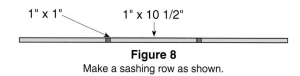

**Figure 8**
Make a sashing row as shown.

3. Join three blocks with two 1" x 10½" strips to make block rows referring to Figure 9 for block positioning in rows.

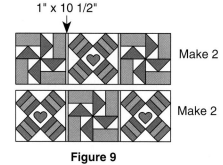

**Figure 9**
Make block rows as shown.

4. Join the block rows with the sashing rows to complete pieced center, referring to the Placement Diagram for positioning of rows; press.

5. Sew a 1" x 31½" strip yellow solid to the top and bottom of the pieced center; press. Sew a 1" x 1" red print square to each end of the 1" x 42" strips yellow solid. Sew these strips to opposite long sides of the pieced center; press.

6. Cut two strips each 5" x 32½" and 5" x 43" animal print and four squares red print 5" x 5".

7. Sew the 5" x 32½" strips animal print to the top

and bottom of the pieced center; press. Sew a 5" x 5" red print square to each end of the 5" x 43" strips animal print. Sew strips to opposite long sides of the pieced center; press.

8. Cut a 45" x 56" piece quilter's fleece and sandwich between completed top and prepared backing piece. Pin or baste layers together to hold flat.

9. Using clear nylon monofilament in the top of the machine and white all-purpose thread in the bobbin, machine-quilt in the seam around the white triangles and squares in the blocks and on the outside seam of the yellow solid sashing strips. Topstitch around outside of quilt ⅛" from edge; trim excess fleece and backing.

10. Hand-quilt down the center of each yellow solid sashing strip using red hand-quilting thread.

11. Using hot pumpkin rayon color twist thread in the top of the machine and spark gold all-purpose thread in the bobbin, stitch a decorative machine buttonhole stitch around each heart shape.

12. Hand-quilt around each heart shape using white hand-quilting thread.

13. When quilting is complete, bind edges with atom red wide bias tape, mitering corners and overlapping ends. Turn the bias tape to the backside; hand-stitch in place with atom red all-purpose thread to finish. ❖

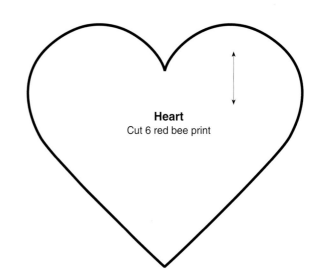

**Heart**
Cut 6 red bee print

# Tropical Delight

BY MICHELE CRAWFORD

If you're headed for the beach with your beach baby, be sure to take this bright colored quilt, and your baby won't lose his special spot. A beach print fabric can be used to make strips and squares, but what really will enchant your little fisherman are the appliquéd fishes that swim across the quilt.

## Tropical Delight

### Project Specifications
Quilt Size: 47" x 47"
Block Size: 12" x 12"
Number of Blocks: 5 A blocks; 4 B blocks

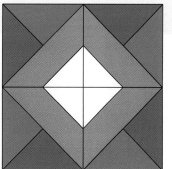

**Block A**
12" x 12"

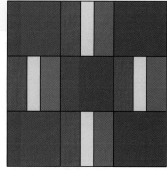

**Block B**
12" x 12"

### Fabric & Batting
- ¼ yard each yellow, blue and purple prints
- ¼ yard bright yellow solid
- ½ yard each white-on-white and green prints
- ⅔ yard each orange and beach prints
- Backing 51" x 51"
- Batting 51" x 51"

### Supplies & Tools
- 1 spool each white, yale blue, rose pink, emerald, tango and spark gold all-purpose thread
- 1 spool each yale blue, dark orange and red rose machine-quilting and craft thread

- 1 spool pinata color-twist rayon thread
- 2 packages spark gold wide bias tape
- 1 skein black embroidery floss
- ¼ yard fusible transfer web
- Basic sewing tools and supplies, soft lead pencil, rotary cutter, ruler and cutting mat

### Instructions
*Note: Use a ¼" seam allowance and all-purpose thread colors to match fabrics for all stitching unless otherwise directed.* Join pieces with right sides together and raw edges even using matching all-purpose thread. Press seam allowances toward

# Tropical Delight

3 1/2" x 40"

3 1/2"
x
3 1/2"

1" x 38"

**Tropical Delight**
Placement Diagram
47" x 47"

the darkest fabrics. When machine quilting, use machine-quilting and craft thread in the bobbin and in the top of the machine.

1. To make Block A, cut 10 squares white-on-white print 3⅞" x 3⅞". Cut each square in half on one diagonal to make 20 W triangles.

2. Cut five squares green print 7¼" x 7¼". Cut each square in half on both diagonals to make 20 G triangles. Repeat with blue print to make 20 B triangles.

3. Prepare template for piece A; cut as directed on the piece.

4. Sew W to A; repeat for four units. Sew B to G as shown in Figure 1; repeat for four units. Sew a B-G unit to a W-A unit as shown in Figure 2 to complete one block unit; repeat for four block units and press. Join four block units to complete one Block A referring to the block drawing; repeat for five blocks and press.

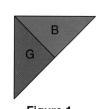

**Figure 1**
Sew B to G as shown.

**Figure 2**
Sew a B-G unit to a W-A unit.

5. To make Block B, cut two strips each green and purple prints 2" by fabric width. Cut two strips yellow print 1½" by fabric width.

6. Sew a yellow print strip between a green and a purple print strip; repeat for two strip sets and press.

7. Cut strip sets into 4½" segments; you will need 16 segments.

8. Cut three strips beach print 4½" by fabric width. Subcut each strip into 4½" segments. You will need 20 segments.

9. Arrange four pieced segments with five beach print squares to make rows as shown in Figure 3. Join in rows; join rows to complete one Block B. Repeat for four blocks and press.

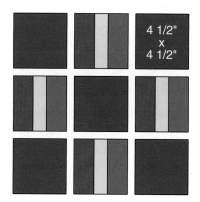

**Figure 3**
Arrange 4 pieced segments with 5 beach print squares.

10. Cut 12 strips white-on-white print 1½" x 12½" for sashing. Cut eight squares orange print 1½" x 1½" for sashing squares.

11. Join two A blocks and one B block with two sashing strips to make a row as shown in Figure 4; repeat for two rows. Press seams toward strips.

# Tropical Delight

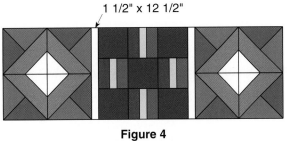

**Figure 4**
Join 2 A blocks and 1 B block with 2
sashing strips to make a row.

12. Join two B blocks and one A block with two sashing strips to make a row as shown in Figure 5; press seams toward strips.

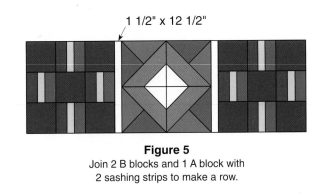

**Figure 5**
Join 2 B blocks and 1 A block with
2 sashing strips to make a row.

13. Join three sashing strips with two sashing squares to make a sashing row as shown in Figure 6; repeat for two rows and press.

14. Join the block rows with the sashing rows to complete the pieced center referring to the Placement Diagram.

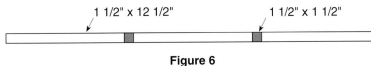

**Figure 6**
Join 3 sashing strips with 2 sashing squares to make a sashing row.

15. Cut four strips white-on-white print 1½" x 38½". Sew a strip to opposite sides of the pieced center; press seams toward strips. Sew a sashing square to each end of each remaining strip. Sew to the remaining sides of the pieced center; press seams toward strips.

16. Cut four strips beach print 4" x 40½" and four squares orange print 4" x 4". Sew a beach print strip to two opposite sides of the pieced center; press seams toward strips. Sew an orange print square to each end of the remaining two strips. Sew a strip to remaining sides of the pieced center; press seams toward strips.

17. Sandwich batting between completed top and prepared backing piece. Pin or baste layers together to hold flat.

18. Using dark orange machine-quilting and craft thread, machine-quilt in the seam around the orange pieces in each A block and the small and large orange print squares. Using yale blue thread, machine-quilt in the seams between the squares in each B block. Using red rose thread and a machine buttonhole or blanket stitch, stitch on each side of the white sashing strips and white border. Topstitch around the outside of the quilt top ⅛" from edge. Trim edges even.

**19.** Bind edges with spark gold wide bias tape.

**20.** Cut a 4" x 12" piece bright yellow solid and a 2½" x 12" piece purple print. Cut the same size pieces fusible transfer web. Bond fusible transfer web to the wrong side of the fabric pieces.

**21.** Prepare templates for fish pieces using pattern given. Trace shapes on the paper side of the fused fabrics as directed on the pattern for number and color to cut. Cut out shapes on traced lines; remove paper backing.

**22.** Center a fish motif in each A block; fuse in place. Using rose pink all-purpose thread in the bobbin and pinata rayon color twist thread in the top of the machine, zigzag-stitch around and inside shapes referring to detail lines on pattern.

**23.** Using a soft lead pencil, lightly trace an eye and mouth on each fish. Using 4 strands black embroidery floss, sew French knots for eyes and backstitch mouths to finish. ❖

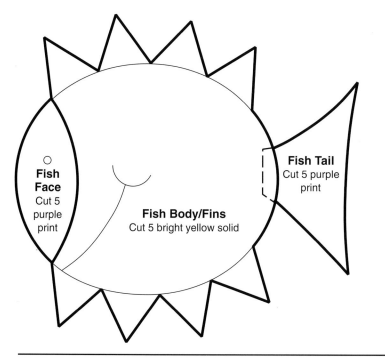

**Fish Face**
Cut 5 purple print

**Fish Body/Fins**
Cut 5 bright yellow solid

**Fish Tail**
Cut 5 purple print

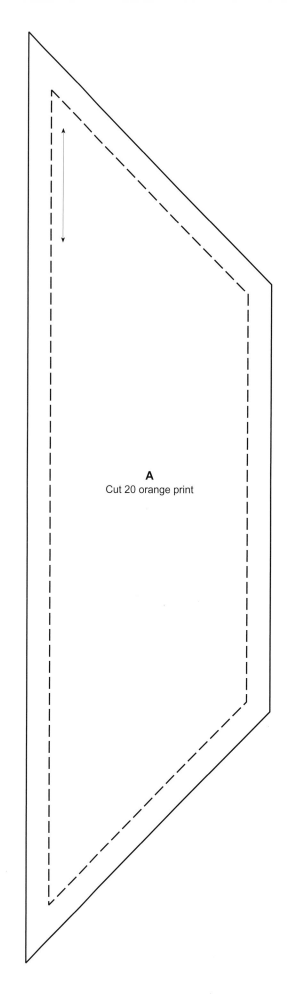

**A**
Cut 20 orange print

# Child's Play

BY SUE HARVEY

A wonderful kids' print and an enchanting animal print were the inspiration for this quilt. Any print that has kids cavorting will be perfect, and you can pick your favorite animals for the animal strips. No matter what your choices, this quilt will make a welcome addition to any child's room and, because it will go together so easily, you'll think it really is child's play.

# Child's Play

**Child's Play**
Placement Diagram
56" x 76"

# Child's Play

## Project Specifications

Quilt Size: 56" x 76"

Block Size: 10" x 10"

Number of Blocks: 24

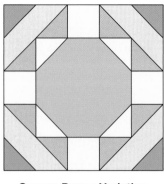

**Square Dance Variation**
10" x 10" Block

## Fabric & Batting

- 1 yard each animal and peach prints
- 1 yard green dot
- 1½ yards cream print
- 2 yards kids print
- Backing 60" x 80"
- Batting 60" x 80"
- 7¾ yards self-made or purchased binding

## Supplies & Tools

- All-purpose thread to match fabrics
- Basic sewing tools and supplies, rotary cutter, mat and ruler

## Instructions

1. Cut two strips 4½" x 64½" along length of kids print; set aside for borders.

2. Cut six strips 6½" by remaining fabric width kids print; subcut into 6½" square segments for A. You will need 28 A squares.

3. Cut 13 strips 2½" by fabric width cream print; subcut into 2½" square segments for B. You will need 208 B squares.

4. Cut two strips each cream and peach prints 5¼" by fabric width; subcut each strip into 5¼" square segments. Cut each square on both diagonals to make F triangles; you will need 50 cream and 54 peach F triangles.

5. Cut four squares 2⅞" x 2⅞" cream print. Cut each square on one diagonal to make G triangles; you will need eight G triangles.

6. Cut six strips animal print 4⅞" by fabric width; subcut into 4⅞" square segments. Cut each square on one diagonal to make C triangles; you will need 96 C triangles.

7. Cut six strips green dot 2½" by fabric width;

# Child's Play

subcut into 2½" square segments for D. You will need 96 D squares.

8. Cut seven strips 2⅞" by fabric width peach print; subcut into 2⅞" square segments. Cut each square on one diagonal to make E triangles; you will need 192 E triangles.

9. Draw a diagonal line on the wrong side of each D square and 112 B squares.

10. Place a B square right sides together on one corner of A. Stitch on the marked line; trim seam allowance to ¼" and press B open as shown in Figure 1. Repeat on all corners of A to make one A-B unit as shown in Figure 2.

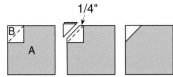

**Figure 1**
Place B on 1 corner of A. Stitch, trim seam allowance and press B open.

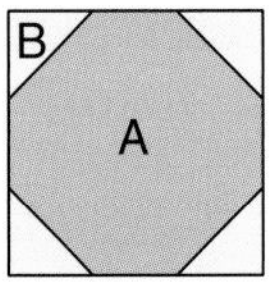

**Figure 2**
Repeat on all corners of A to make 1 A-B unit.

11. Repeat step 10 to make 28 A-B units. *Note: Set aside four A-B units for border corners.*

12. Place a D square right sides together on the right-angle corner of C as shown in Figure 3. Stitch, trim and press to complete one C-D unit as shown in Figure 4. Repeat for 96 C-D units.

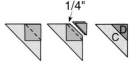

**Figure 3**
Place D on the right-angle corner of C.

**Figure 4**
Stitch, trim and press to complete 1 C-D unit.

13. Sew E to opposite sides of B as shown in Figure 5; repeat for 96 B-E units.

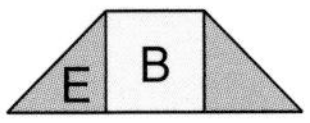

**Figure 5**
Sew E to opposite sides of B.

14. Sew a B-E unit to each side of an A-B unit as shown in Figure 6. Add a C-D unit to each angled side of the pieced unit to complete one Square Dance Variation block, again referring to Figure 6; repeat for 24 blocks.

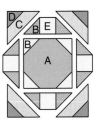

**Figure 6**
Sew a B-E unit to each side of an A-B unit; add C-D to each angled side to complete 1 block.

15. Join four blocks to make a row; repeat for six rows. Join rows to complete the pieced center.

16. Cut (and piece) two strips each 2½" x 44½" and 2½" x 60½" green dot. Sew the longer strips to opposite long sides of the pieced center and shorter strips to top and bottom.

17. Join 11 peach and 10 cream F triangles on short sides as shown in Figure 7; add a G triangle to each end, again referring to Figure 7. Repeat to make two F-G strips.

**Figure 7**
Join 11 peach and 10 cream F triangles; add G to each end.

18. Cut and piece two strips 4½" x 44½" kids print. Sew a strip to the peach side of one F-G strip referring to the Placement Diagram for positioning; repeat for second strip. Sew a strip to the top and bottom of the pieced center.

19. Join 16 peach and 15 cream F triangles as shown in Figure 8; add a G triangle to each end, again referring to Figure 8. Repeat for two F-G strips.

**Figure 8**
Join 16 peach and 15 cream F triangles; add G to each end.

20. Sew a kids print strip cut in step 1 to the peach side of one F-G strip; repeat for second strip. Sew an A-B unit to each end of each strip referring to the Placement Diagram for positioning. Sew a strip to opposite long sides to complete pieced top.

21. Sandwich batting between pieced top and prepared backing piece; pin or baste to hold.

22. Hand- or machine-quilt as desired. *Note: The sample shown was professionally machine-quilted.*

23. Trim backing and batting even with top; remove pins or basting.

24. Bind with self-made or purchased binding to finish. ❖

# Scrap-Chain Quilt

BY NANCY BRENAN DANIEL

What fun! Start with a juvenile cream print and add bright-colored fabric scraps that have been collecting in your fabric stash, and you can create a quilt that would delight any child. If the cream print is a directional print, be sure that the rectangles are cut in the same vertical direction. While the cream print in the photographed quilt is actually a directional print, the bears don't stand out because the print is not bright. If your juvenile print is a bright one, be careful when cutting your fabric. Additional fabric may be required to keep all of the bears going in the same direction.

## Project Specifications
Quilt Size: 47" x 67"

## Fabric & Batting
- ⅜ yard blue stripe
- ¾ yard red print
- 1¾ yards cream print
- 192 bright-colored scrap squares 2½" x 2½" for F
- 8 bright-colored print scrap squares 2⅞" x 2⅞" for G
- Backing 51" x 71"
- Batting 51" x 71"
- 6¾ yards self-made or purchased binding

## Supplies & Tools
- Neutral color all-purpose thread
- Clear nylon monofilament
- Basic sewing tools and supplies, rotary cutter, mat and ruler

## Instructions
1. Cut two strips cream print 2½" x 56½" along length of print for side inside border strips; set aside.

2. Cut the following rectangles from the cream print: four 2½" x 6½" for A; six 2½" x 8½" for B; six 4½" x 6½" for C; nine 4½" x 8½" for D; and sixteen 4½" x 12½" for E.

3. Cut eight squares each cream print and bright-colored scraps 2⅞" x 2⅞"; subcut each square on one diagonal to make G triangles.

# Scrap-Chain Quilt

3 1/2" x 40"

2" x 36"

2" x 32"

3 1/2" x 67"

2" x 60"

2" x 56"

**Scrap-Chain Quilt**
Placement Diagram
47" x 67"

4. Sew a cream print G to a scrap G along the diagonal to make a G unit as shown in Figure 1; repeat for all G triangles.

5. Join two G units to create a G-G unit as shown in Figure 2; repeat for eight G-G units. Set aside.

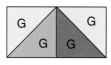

**Figure 1**
Sew a cream print G to a scrap G along the diagonal to make a G unit.

**Figure 2**
Join 2 G units to create a G-G unit.

6. Draw a line on the diagonal of each F square. Place an F square on one corner of A; stitch on the diagonal line as shown in Figure 3. Trim excess ¼" beyond seam line as shown in Figure 4.

7. Flip F back and press to make an A1 unit as shown in Figure 5; repeat for two units.

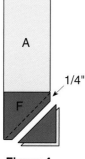

**Figure 3**
Place an F square on 1 corner of A; stitch on the diagonal line.

**Figure 4**
Trim excess 1/4" beyond seam line.

**Figure 5**
Flip F back and press to make an A1 unit.

8. Repeat steps 6 and 7 with F and A to make two A2 units as shown in Figure 6.

9. Repeat this process with B, C, D and E rectangles and F squares referring to Figure 7 for positioning of F squares and number to make for each unit.

**Figure 6**
Make an A2 unit as shown.

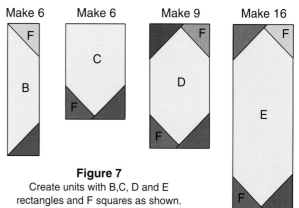

Make 6   Make 6   Make 9   Make 16

**Figure 7**
Create units with B,C, D and E rectangles and F squares as shown.

10. Join two F squares as shown in Figure 8; repeat for eight F1 units.

**Figure 8**
Join 2 F squares to make an F1 unit.

**Figure 9**
Join 4 F squares to make a Four-Patch unit.

# Scrap-Chain Quilt

**11.** Join four F squares to make a Four-Patch unit as shown in Figure 9; repeat for 12 Four-Patch units.

**12.** Join units as shown in Figure 10 to make rows; press seams in one direction.

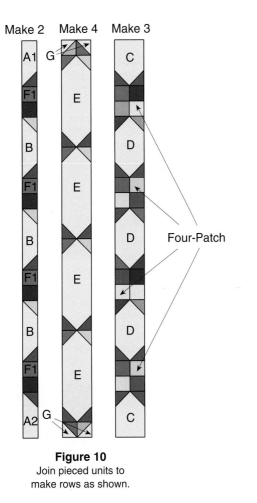

Make 2     Make 4     Make 3

Four-Patch

**Figure 10**
Join pieced units to
make rows as shown.

**13.** Join rows to complete pieced center referring to the Placement Diagram for positioning of rows; press seams in one direction.

**14.** Cut two strips cream print 2½" x 32½" along width of fabric. Sew strips to the top and bottom of the pieced center. Sew the vertical strips cut in step 1 to the opposite long sides; press seams toward strips.

**15.** Cut (and piece as necessary) two strips each blue stripe 2½" x 36½" and 2½" x 60½". Sew the shorter strips to the top and bottom and longer strips to opposite sides; press seams toward strips.

**16.** Cut (and piece as necessary) two strips each red print 4" x 40½" and 4" x 67½". Sew the shorter strips to the top and bottom and longer strips to opposite sides; press seams toward strips.

**17.** Sandwich batting between the completed top and prepared backing piece; pin or baste layers together to hold flat.

**18.** Quilt as desired by hand or machine.
*Note: The quilt shown was machine-quilted in the ditch of seams between rows and border strips and a meandering design on border strips using clear nylon monofilament in the top of the machine and all-purpose thread in the bobbin.*

**19.** When quilting is complete, remove pins or basting; trim edges even. Bind with self-made or purchased binding to complete the quilt. ❖

# Mouse to Tower

BY LINDA DENNER

The husband of this quilt's designer is a small-plane pilot, and she imagines that flying is a dream of all men young and old. With this in mind, she's created a cheery little quilt that is fun to make, using some of those accumulated scraps. If this quilt is too small for your little flyer, add more borders to increase the size of your finished quilt.

## Project Specifications
Quilt Size: 34" x 40"

## Fabric & Batting
- 18½" x 18½" square blue solid for background
- 1 yard print for outer border
- 84 assorted 3½" x 3½" squares in a variety of shades of red, white and blue
- Scraps for appliqué
- Backing 38" x 44"
- Batting 38" x 44"
- ½ yard red print for binding

## Supplies & Tools
- 1 spool neutral color all-purpose thread
- 1 spool quilting thread
- 1 skein black embroidery floss
- 1 red fabric crayon
- Basic sewing supplies and tools, rotary cutter, mat and ruler, tracing paper or freezer paper

## Instructions
1. Arrange twenty-four 3½" squares in four rows of six squares each; join squares in rows. Sew two stitched rows to opposite sides of the 18½" x 18½" square as shown in Figure 1.

**Figure 1**
Sew strips to sides.

# Mouse to Tower

2. Arrange 60 squares in six rows of 10 squares each; join squares in rows. Sew three stitched rows to the top and bottom of the 18½" x 18½" square as shown in Figure 2.

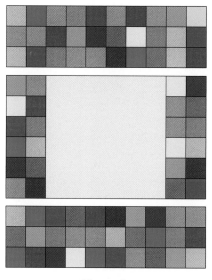

**Figure 2**
Sew strips to top and bottom.

3. Trace individual appliqué pieces on tracing paper or freezer paper using full-size pattern drawing given. Dotted lines on pattern indicate where pieces overlap. Trace the patterns onto chosen fabric scraps on the right side of the fabric for freezer-paper method or on the wrong side of fabrics for traditional appliqué methods.

4. Cut out shapes, adding a ¼" seam allowance when cutting for hand appliqué.

5. Position pieces on center square, layering as necessary, referring to the Placement Diagram and photo of project for arrangement.

6. Appliqué in place by hand or machine using thread to match fabrics.

7. Embroider facial features on the mouse using 1 strand of black embroidery floss—satin-stitch eyes and nose, stem-stitch mouth. Use fabric crayon to apply shading to face. *Note: Blush makeup may be substituted for fabric crayon.*

8. Cut two strips each border fabric 2½" x 36½" and 2½" x 34½". Sew the longer strips to opposite sides of the pieced center and the shorter strips to the top and bottom; press seams toward strips.

9. Sandwich batting between the completed top and prepared backing piece. Pin or baste layers together to hold flat.

10. Quilt as desired by hand or machine. *Note: The sample is quilted with clouds and air currents.*

11. When quilting is complete, trim edges even and remove pins or basting.

12. Bind edges with 1½"-wide self-made binding from red print to finish. ❖

# Mouse to Tower

**Mouse to Tower**
Placement Diagram
34" x 40"

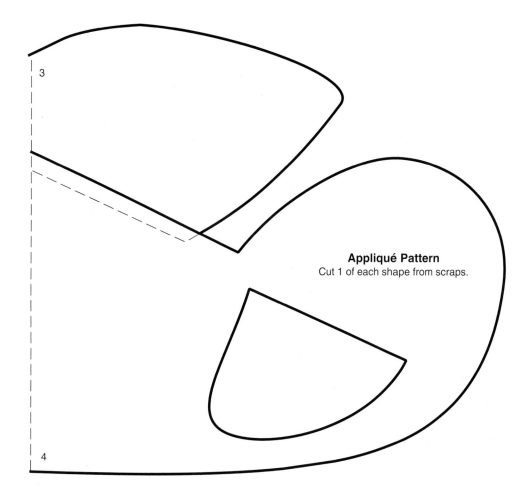

**Appliqué Pattern**
Cut 1 of each shape from scraps.

3

4

# Mouse to Tower

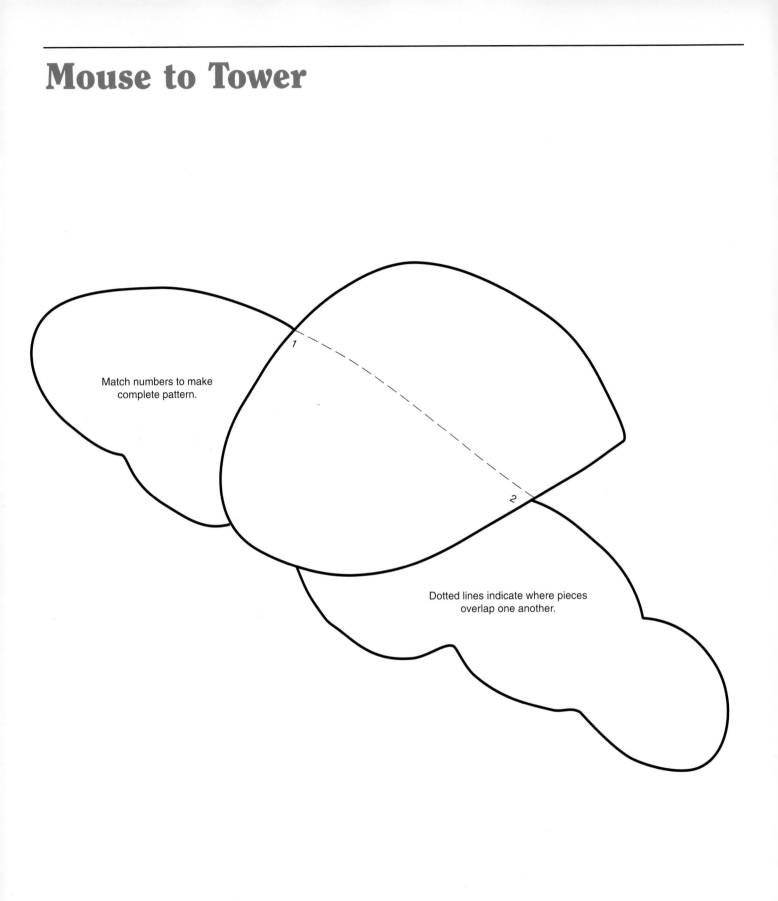

Match numbers to make
complete pattern.

1

2

Dotted lines indicate where pieces
overlap one another.

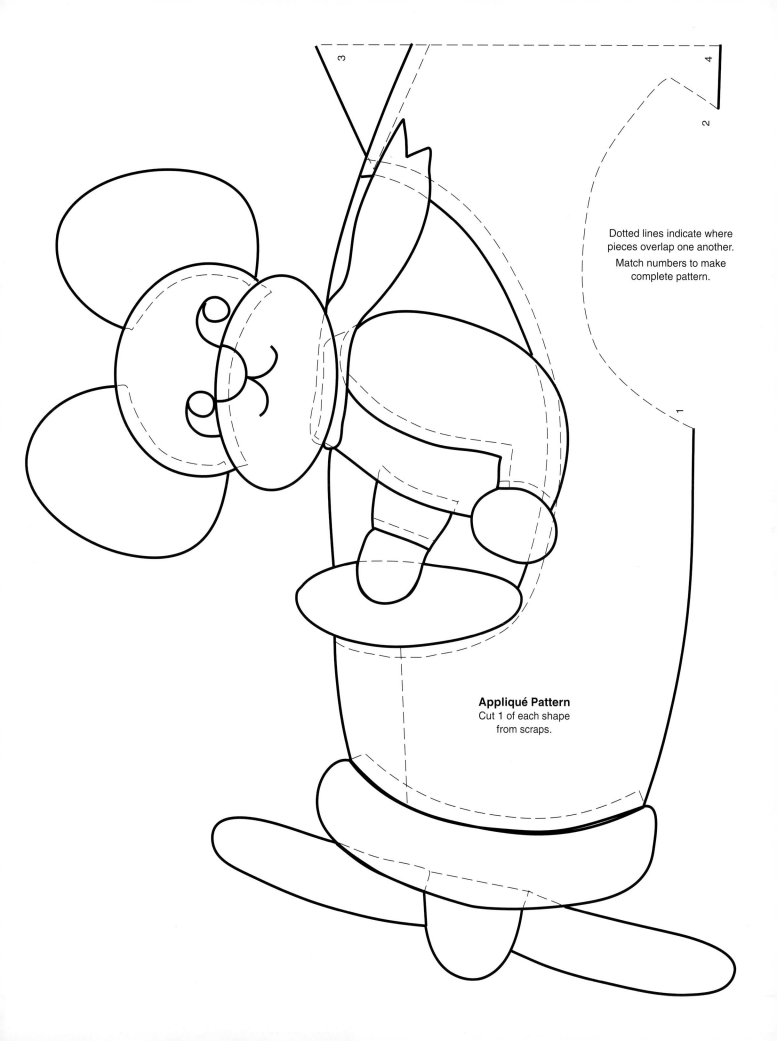

Dotted lines indicate where pieces overlap one another.

Match numbers to make complete pattern.

**Appliqué Pattern**
Cut 1 of each shape from scraps.

# Easter Baby Quilt

BY MICHELE CRAWFORD

Imagine how delighted your special baby will be when she sees that the Easter Bunny has brought her own special Easter quilt! If the bunnies don't show your love, the hearts certainly will. If you don't want to make an Easter quilt, just substitute another print for the bunny squares and strips. Just be sure to keep the hearts!

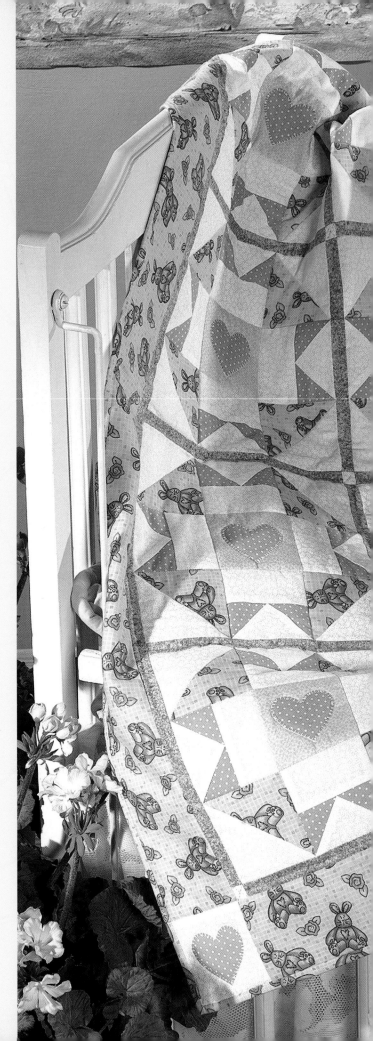

# Easter Baby Quilt

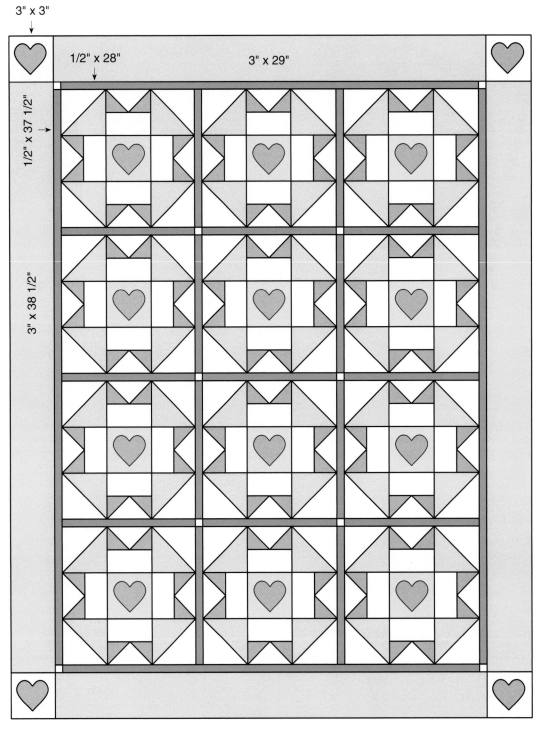

3" x 3"

1/2" x 28"

3" x 29"

1/2" x 37 1/2"

3" x 38 1/2"

**Easter Baby Quilt**
Placement Diagram
35" x 44 1/2"

# Easter Baby Quilt

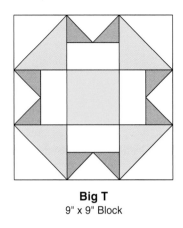

**Big T**
9" x 9" Block

## Project Specifications

Quilt Size: 35" x 44½"

Block Size: 9" x 9"

Number of Blocks: 12

## Fabric & Batting

- ⅛ yard yellow print
- ⅙ yard pink bunny print
- ⅓ yard green print
- ⅓ yard pink dot
- ¾ yard yellow bunny print
- 1 yard white print
- Backing 39" x 49"
- 1½ yards quilter's fleece

## Supplies & Tools

- White all-purpose thread
- White, salmon and pale yellow quilting thread
- ¼ yard fusible transfer web
- Basic sewing tools and supplies, rotary cutter, mat and ruler

## Instructions

1. Cut 24 squares yellow bunny print 3⅞" x 3⅞"; cut each square in half on one diagonal to make 48 B triangles.

2. Cut 12 squares yellow print 3½" x 3½" for Y.

3. Cut 48 squares pink dot 2⅜" x 2⅜"; cut each square on one diagonal to make 96 P triangles.

4. Cut 12 squares 4¼" x 4¼" white print; cut each square on both diagonals to make T triangles. Cut 48 rectangles white print 2" x 3½" for W. Cut 24 squares white print 3⅞" x 3⅞"; cut each square in half on one diagonal to make 48 WT triangles.

5. Sew WT to B; repeat for four units. Sew P to two adjacent sides of T; sew W to the P side. Repeat for four units.

6. Arrange the pieced units in rows with Y referring to Figure 1. Join units in rows; join rows to complete one block. Repeat for 12 blocks.

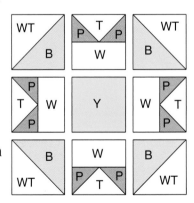

**Figure 1**
Arrange the pieced units in rows with Y.

7. Cut the following from green print: 17 strips 1" x 9½"; two strips 1" x 28½"; and two strips 1" x 38".

8. Cut 10 squares white print 1" x 1".

9. Join three 1" x 9½" green print strips with two 1" x 1" white print squares to make a sashing row as shown in Figure 2; repeat for three sashing rows. Press seams toward strips.

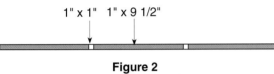

1" x 1"  1" x 9 1/2"

**Figure 2**
Make a sashing row as shown.

10. Join three pieced blocks with two 1" x 9½" green print strips to make a block row as shown in Figure 3; repeat for four block rows. Press seams toward strips.

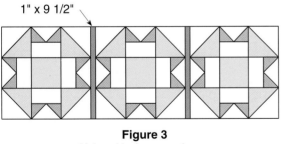

1" x 9 1/2"

**Figure 3**
Make a block row as shown.

11. Join the block rows with the sashing rows to complete the pieced center; press seams in one direction.

12. Sew a 1" x 28½" strip green print to the top and bottom; press seams toward strips. Sew a 1" x 1" square white print to each end of the 1" x 38" strips green print; press seams toward strips. Sew the strips to opposite long sides of the pieced center; press seams toward strips.

13. Cut four squares white print 3½" x 3½" and two strips each yellow bunny print 3½" x 29½" and 3½" x 39".

14. Sew a 3½" x 29½" strip yellow bunny print to the top and bottom of the pieced center. Sew a 3½" x 3½" square white print to each end of the 3½" x 39" strips yellow bunny print; press seams toward strips. Sew a strip to opposite long sides of the pieced center; press seams toward strips.

15. Prepare template for heart shape using pattern given. Bond fusible transfer web to the wrong side of the pink dot. Trace 16 heart shapes on the paper side of the fused fabric; cut out heart shapes on traced lines. Remove paper backing.

16. Center a heart on the Y square of each pieced block; fuse in place. Center and fuse a heart on each white print corner square.

17. Using white quilting thread in the top of the machine and white all-purpose thread in the bobbin, stitch a machine buttonhole stitch around each heart shape.

18. Cut a piece of quilter's fleece 39" x 49". Sandwich fleece between completed top and prepared backing piece. Pin or baste layers together to hold flat.

19. Using pale yellow quilting thread in the top of the machine and white all-purpose thread in the bobbin, machine-quilt in the seams of all yellow bunny print triangles and yellow print squares and in the ditch of the green print border seams.

20. Hand-quilt down the center of each print border strip using salmon quilting thread.

21. When quilting is complete, trim edges even. Cut four strips pink bunny print 1¼" by fabric width. Sew together on short ends with right sides together to make one long strip. Press one long edge under ¼".

22. Sew the binding strip right sides together with quilt top, mitering corners and overlapping ends. Turn the binding to the backside of the quilt; hand-stitch in place to finish. ❖

**Heart**
Cut 16 pink dot

# Ruffles & Bows

BY TESS HERLAN

If you are looking for a baby quilt that is quick to make but has a little extra love in it, this is the perfect quilt. Find a cute print for the squares such as the bunny print in this quilt. The hearts in that bunny print inspired the appliquéd hearts on the quilt, but you'll want to add hearts no matter what print you use. The ruffles, eyelet and ribbons just seem to add something special for that extra-special baby.

**Ruffles & Bows**
Placement Diagram
38" x 46" without ruffle

# Ruffles & Bows

## Project Specifications

Quilt Size: 38" x 46" without ruffle

Block Size: 4" x 4"

Number of Blocks: 42

## Fabric & Batting

- ¾ yard each blue print and muslin
- 1¼ yards pink print
- 1¾ yards coordinating print
- Backing 42" x 50"
- Batting 42" x 50"

## Supplies & Tools

- Neutral color all-purpose thread
- 5 yards beaded lace eyelet
- 7 yards ¼"-wide blue satin ribbon
- Heavy paper
- Basic sewing supplies and tools

## Making Quilt Top

1. Cut six strips each pink and blue prints 2½" by fabric width.

2. Sew a pink strip to a blue strip with right sides together along length; repeat for all pink and blue strips. Press seams toward darker fabric.

**Four-Patch**
4" x 4" Block

3. Cut each stitched strip into 2½" segments.

4. Join two segments cut in step 3 to make a Four-Patch block as shown in Figure 1. Repeat for 42 blocks.

**Figure 1**
Join stitched segments to make a Four-Patch block.

5. Cut five strips coordinating print 4½" by fabric width. Cut each strip into 4½" segments for 39 squares.

6. Arrange Four-Patch blocks with print squares to make rows, beginning six rows with a Four-Patch block and three rows with a print square. Arrange seven rows together referring to Figure 2. Join these rows.

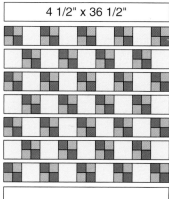

**Figure 2**
Arrange units to make rows.

7. Cut two strips muslin 4½" x 36½". Sew a strip to the top and bottom of the pieced row section.

8. Sew a pieced row to the top and bottom of the section as shown in Figure 3.

9. Cut two strips each muslin 1½" x 38½" and 1½" x 44½". Sew the longer strips to opposite sides and the shorter strips to the top and bottom of the pieced section, again referring to Figure 3.

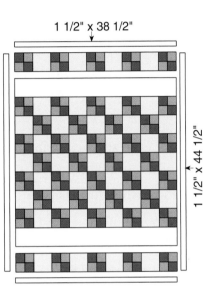

1 1/2" x 38 1/2"

1 1/2" x 44 1/2"

**Figure 3**
Sew a pieced row to the top and bottom. Add 1 1/2"-wide muslin strips as shown.

## Making Hearts

1. Make 12 paper templates using heart pattern given. Cut fabric pieces as directed on piece, adding a ¼" seam allowance all around when cutting.

2. Baste the hearts to the paper template by starting about ½" above the point, folding seam allowance over paper and basting through the paper until you reach the deepest part of the curve.

3. Stitch a small running stitch on the seam line through the curve to the inside point. *Note: You should only be stitching through one layer of fabric. Nothing has been folded yet.* Clip the fabric into the point, stopping about ¹⁄₁₆" from the paper. Take one basting stitch below the point through the fabric and paper, pulling thread tightly. Fabric will wrap around the curved edge of the paper as shown in Figure 4.

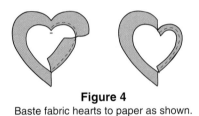

**Figure 4**
Baste fabric hearts to paper as shown.

4. Once again stitch a running stitch through the fabric only around the second curve. Baste through both the fabric and the paper, pulling thread tightly to shape the fabric around the second curve; baste to point.

5. Fold seam allowance over paper to form the point; baste around the point to the starting place. Take one extra basting stitch past the starting point; clip thread. *Note: It is not necessary to fasten thread with a knot.*

6. Position hearts on muslin strip, centering above the second, third, fourth, sixth, seventh and eighth

blocks. *Hint: Put a small amount of fabric glue on the seam allowance on the wrong side of the heart; lightly press with fingertips. This should hold hearts for appliqué without the need to pin.*

7. Appliqué hearts in place with paper inside; press. Turn quilt top over; cut inside the appliqué lines to remove the background fabric and see the papers. Pull basting threads; remove papers from the back.

### Making Mock Ruffle

1. Cut six strips pink print 3" by width of fabric. Cut six strips coordinating print 5" by width of fabric. Sew a print strip to a coordinating print strip with right sides together along length; repeat for six strip sets. Press seams toward darker fabric.

2. Join pieced strips together on short ends to make a large tube. Fold in half with wrong sides together; press, having raw edges even; 1" of coordinating print fabric will show on the right side above the pink print.

3. Run a gathering stitch along the raw edges. Attach to quilt top, adjusting the fullness of the ruffle evenly on all sides. Be sure there is enough fullness at the corners so the ruffle lies flat.

### Finishing

1. Sew the beaded lace eyelet to the narrow muslin-strip border, having the edges next to the seam lines on the quilt top.

2. Weave the ribbon through the eyelet. Add ribbon bows at the corner and at the center of the appliquéd rows.

3. Lay backing piece wrong side up; place batting on top with quilt top right side up on top of batting. Pin or baste layers together. Tie or quilt by hand or machine to hold layers together. *Note: The sample quilt was hand-quilted through the center of the blocks on a diagonal line. Each heart was outline-quilted.*

4. Trim batting only even with outer edge of narrow muslin-strip border. Trim backing to allow ¼" to turn under and sew to the seam line of the ruffle to finish. ❖

**Heart**
Cut 4 each pink, blue and coordinating prints

Add seam allowance when cutting fabric patches.

# Circus Is in Town

BY MICHELE CRAWFORD

Finding two brightly colored circus prints encouraged this designer to create this exciting child's quilt. A clown print was used in half the blocks and a circus print was used in the other half. If clowns and circuses don't appeal to you, try making this quilt with any other theme like teddy bears or toys. Any theme you choose is sure to bring smiles to a child.

# Circus Is in Town

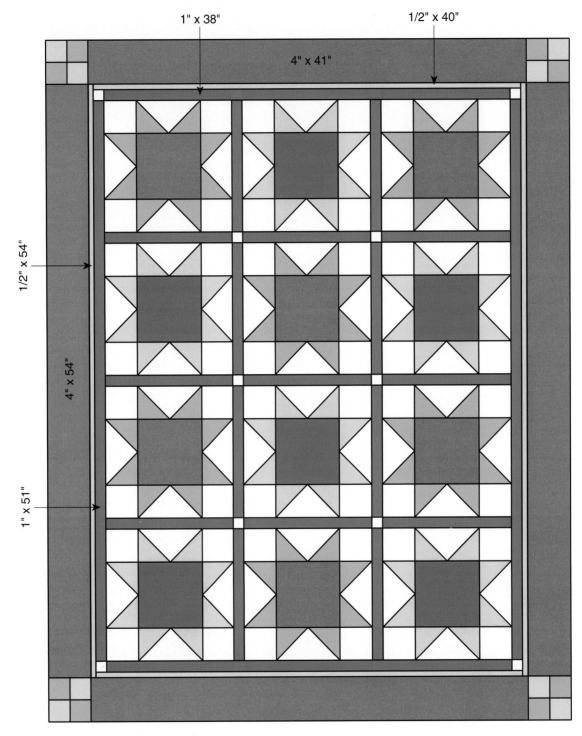

1" x 38"

1/2" x 40"

4" x 41"

1/2" x 54"

4" x 54"

1" x 51"

**Circus Is in Town**
Placement Diagram
49" x 62"

# Circus Is in Town

## Project Specifications

Quilt Size: 49" x 62"

Block Size: 12" x 12"

Number of Blocks: 12

## Fabric & Batting

- ¼ yard circus print
- ½ yard green mottled
- ⅝ yard blue print
- ⅝ yard yellow solid
- 1 yard clown print
- 1¼ yards white-on-white print
- Backing 53" x 66"
- Batting 53" x 66"
- 6½ yards self-made or purchased binding

## Supplies & Tools

- All-purpose thread to match fabrics
- White, red and green machine-quilting and craft thread
- Basic sewing tools and supplies

## Instructions

1. Prepare templates using pattern pieces given; cut A–D pieces as directed on each piece for one block. Repeat for six yellow and six green blocks. Cut E and F pieces as directed on each piece.

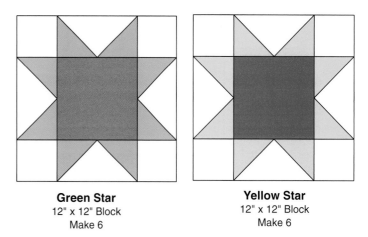

**Green Star**
12" x 12" Block
Make 6

**Yellow Star**
12" x 12" Block
Make 6

2. To piece one block, sew a colored B to each short side of C; repeat for four units.

3. Sew a B-C unit to opposite sides of A (clown print for green blocks and circus print for yellow blocks) as shown in Figure 1.

4. Sew a D square to each end of the remaining B-C units and sew to the pieced unit to complete one block as shown in Figure 2; repeat for six each yellow and green blocks.

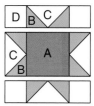

**Figure 1**
Sew a B-C unit to opposite sides of A.

**Figure 2**
Sew a D square to each end of the remaining B-C units and sew to the pieced unit to complete 1 block.

5. Cut 17 strips blue print 1½" x 12½" for sashing. Join one yellow and two green blocks with two sashing strips to make a row as shown in Figure 3;

# Circus Is in Town

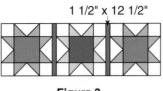

1 1/2" x 12 1/2"

**Figure 3**
Join 1 yellow and 2 green blocks
with 2 sashing strips to make a row.

repeat for two rows. Join one green and two yellow blocks with two sashing strips to make a row; repeat for two rows. Press seams in one direction.

E        1 1/2" x 12 1/2"

**Figure 4**
Join 2 E squares with 3 sashing
strips to make a sashing row.

6. Join two E squares with three sashing strips to make a sashing row as shown in Figure 4; repeat for three sashing rows. Press seams in one direction.

7. Cut (and piece) two strips each 1½" x 38½" and 1½" x 51½" blue print. Sew the shorter strips to the top and bottom of the pieced center. Sew an E square to each end of the remaining strips; sew to opposite long sides of the pieced center. Press seams toward strips.

8. Cut (and piece) two strips each yellow solid 1" x 40½" and 1" x 54½"; sew the shorter strips to the top and bottom and the longer strips to opposite long sides of the pieced center. Press seams toward strips.

9. Sew a yellow solid F to a green mottled F; repeat for eight units. Join two units as shown in Figure 5 to make corner Four-Patch units.

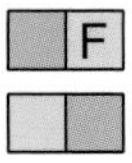

**Figure 5**
Join 2 F units as
shown to make a
corner Four-Patch unit.

10. Cut (and piece) two strips each clown print 4½" x 41½" and 4½" x 54½". Sew the shorter strips to the top and bottom of the pieced center. Sew a corner Four-Patch unit to each end of the remaining strips; sew to opposite long sides of the pieced center. Press seams toward strips.

11. Sandwich batting between completed top and prepared backing piece; pin or baste to hold layers together.

12. Quilt as desired by hand or machine *Note: The quilt shown was machine-quilted in the A, C and D pieces using the designs given and in the border using the star design with machine-quilting and craft thread to match fabrics.*

13. When quilting is complete, trim edges even and remove pins or basting. Bind edges with self-made or purchased binding to finish. ❖

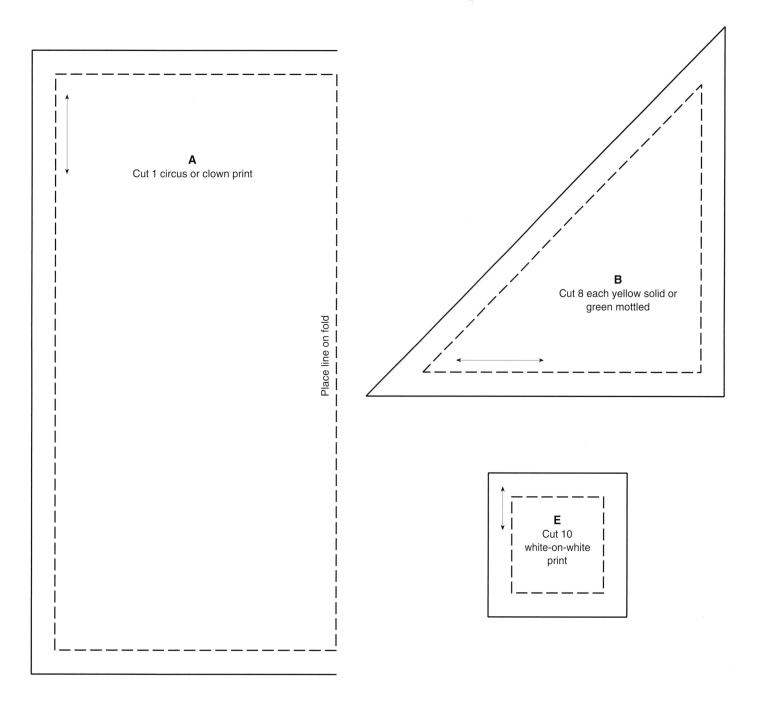

**A**
Cut 1 circus or clown print

Place line on fold

**B**
Cut 8 each yellow solid or
green mottled

**E**
Cut 10
white-on-white
print

# Circus Is in Town

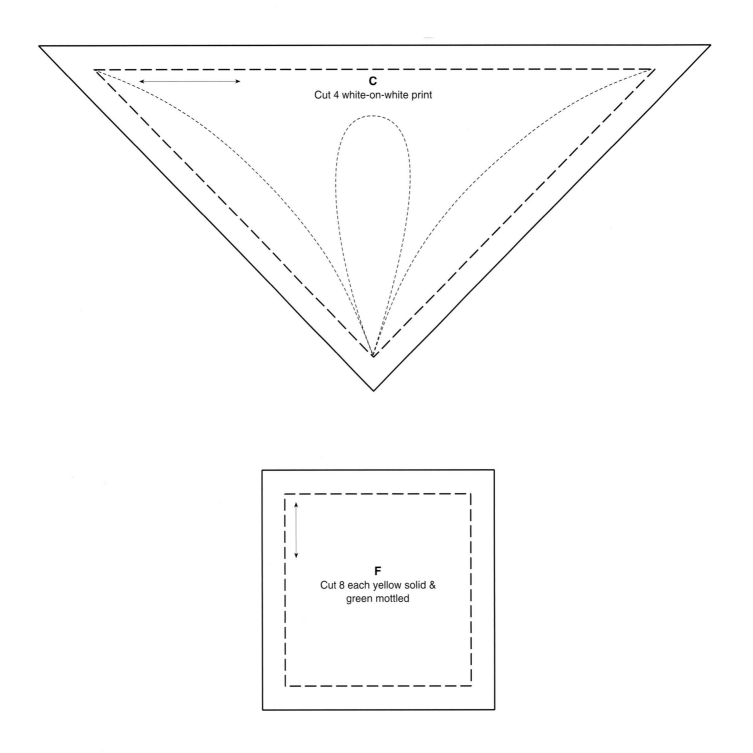

C
Cut 4 white-on-white print

F
Cut 8 each yellow solid &
green mottled

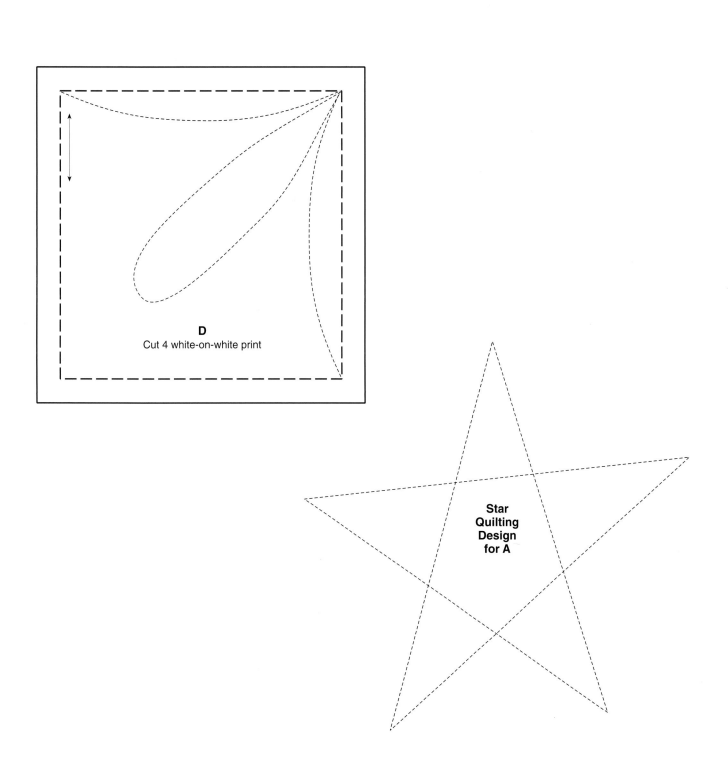

**D**
Cut 4 white-on-white print

**Star
Quilting
Design
for A**

# Mini Sailboats

BY CHERYL FALL

This little sailboat quilt is perfect for that little sailor in your life. It's easy to make and fun to see. Cover a dear child or hang it on a wall in the nursery, and the little one will sail off into dream land.

**Sailboat**
6" x 7" Block

## Project Specifications
Quilt Size: 16" x 18"
Block Size: 6" x 7"
Number of Blocks: 4

## Fabric & Batting
- 2 rectangles 6½" x 7½" each medium blue and dark blue prints
- 2 strips red print 2½" x 14½"
- 2 strips white print 2½" x 12½"
- 4 squares yellow print 2½" x 2½"
- Scraps red, white and yellow prints
- Backing 18" x 20"
- Fusible fleece 18" x 20"

## Supplies & Tools
- 1 spool each natural and blue all-purpose thread
- 1 spool each rayon thread to match appliqué fabrics
- 1 spool clear nylon monofilament
- 1 package blue extra-wide, double-fold bias tape

- 14" x 14" piece fusible transfer web
- Basic sewing tools and supplies

## Instructions
*Note: All seam allowances are ¼" and are included in the measurements given. Appliqué pieces do not require seam allowance for machine appliqué.*

1. Join a medium blue print and dark blue print 6½" x 7½" rectangle on the 6½" sides to make a block row; repeat. Join these two block rows, reversing colors referring to the Placement Diagram.

2. Using patterns given, reverse and trace appliqué shapes onto the paper side of the fusible transfer web. Cut out shapes leaving a margin around each piece.

3. Fuse shapes to the wrong side of appropriate color fabric scraps as directed on each piece.

4. Cut out shapes on marked lines; remove paper backing.

# Mini Sailboats

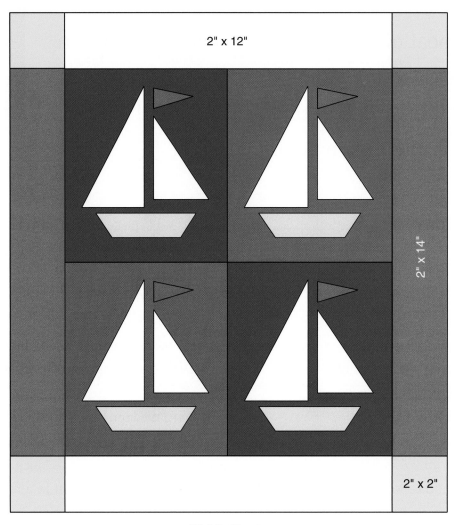

**Mini Sailboats**
Placement Diagram
16" x 18"

5. Arrange one set of sailboat pieces on each stitched rectangle on the pieced section, referring to the Placement Diagram. *Note: The pattern pieces are given in the exact placement to use as a guide for positioning.* Fuse shapes in place following manufacturer's instructions.

6. Sew a 2½" x 14½" red strips to opposite long sides of the fused center; press seams toward strips. Sew a 2½" x 2½" yellow square to each end of the 2½" x 14½" white strips. Sew a strip to the top and bottom of the fused center; press seams toward strips.

7. Fuse fleece to wrong side of pieced top; trim excess.

8. Using thread to match appliqué shapes in the top of the machine and natural all-purpose thread in the bobbin, machine-appliqué shapes in place.

9. Sandwich quilter's fleece between the completed top and the prepared backing piece; pin or baste to hold.

10. Machine-quilt as desired using monofilament in the top of the machine and all-purpose thread in the bobbin. Stitch close to raw edges of quilt top.

11. Trim away excess backing; remove pins or basting. Bind quilt edges with blue bias tape, mitering corners and overlapping ends. ❖

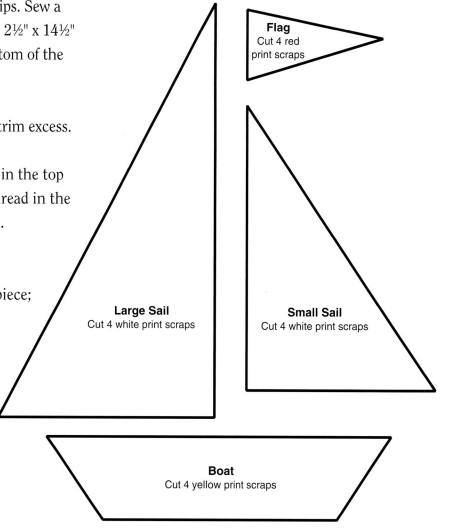

**Flag**
Cut 4 red print scraps

**Large Sail**
Cut 4 white print scraps

**Small Sail**
Cut 4 white print scraps

**Boat**
Cut 4 yellow print scraps

# Bugs on the Nine-Patch

BY DAN & SUSAN SULLIVAN

What kids don't love bugs—often to the dismay of their parents. And what kid is not going to love this quilt that uses bug fabric. If you can't find bug fabric—or if you don't like bugs—just make this quilt using bright fabrics. Later if you decide to take this quilt outside, the bright fabrics will make sure that that the quilt won't get lost in the grass.

# Bugs on the Nine-Patch

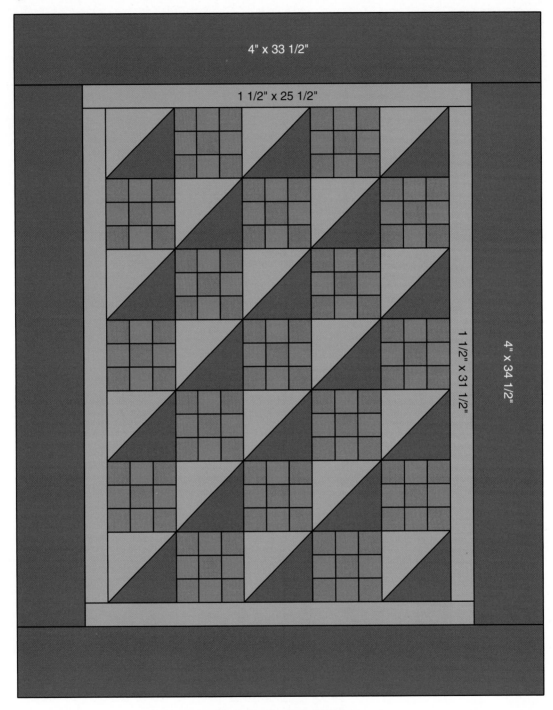

4" x 33 1/2"

1 1/2" x 25 1/2"

1 1/2" x 31 1/2"

4" x 34 1/2"

**Bugs on the Nine-Patch**
Placement Diagram
33 1/2" x 42 1/2"

# Bugs on the Nine-Patch

## Project Specifications

Quilt Size: 33½" x 42½"

Block Size: 4½" x 4½"

Number of Blocks: Nine-Patch—17; Triangle—18

## Fabric & Batting

- ⅓ yard each lime green print and blue check
- ⅔ yard bug print
- 1 yard blue print
- Backing 37" x 46"
- Batting 37" x 46"
- 5 yards self-made or purchased binding

## Supplies & Tools

- All-purpose thread to match fabrics
- Basic sewing tools and supplies

## Instructions

1. Cut four strips blue check and five strips lime green print 2" by fabric width.

2. Sew a blue check strip between two lime green print strips; press seams toward blue check. Repeat for second strip set. Cut strips apart in 2" segments. You will need 34 segments.

3. Sew a lime green print strip between two blue check

**Triangle**
4 1/2" x 4 1/2" Block
Make 18

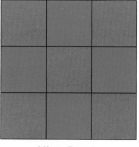

**Nine-Patch**
4 1/2" x 4 1/2" Block
Make 17

strips; press seams toward blue check. Cut strips apart in 2" segments. You will need 17 segments.

4. Join segments as shown in Figure 1 to make a Nine-Patch block; repeat for 17 blocks.

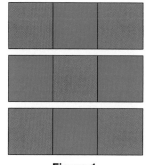

**Figure 1**
Join segments to make
a Nine-Patch block.

5. Cut two strips each blue print and bug print 5⅜" by fabric width. Cut each strip into nine 5⅜" square segments. Cut each square in half on one diagonal to make triangles. You will need 18 of each color triangle.

6. Join a blue print triangle to a bug print triangle to make a Triangle block as shown in Figure 2; repeat for all triangles.

# Bugs on the Nine-Patch

**Figure 2**
Join 2 triangles to make
a Triangle block.

7. Join three Triangle blocks with two Nine-Patch blocks to make a row as shown in Figure 3; repeat for four rows.

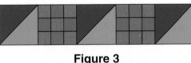

**Figure 3**
Join 3 Triangle blocks with 2
Nine-Patch blocks to make a row.

8. Join three Nine-Patch blocks with two Triangle blocks to make a row as shown in Figure 4; repeat for three rows.

**Figure 4**
Join 3 Nine-Patch blocks with 2
Triangle blocks to make a row.

9. Join the rows referring to the Placement Diagram to complete pieced center; press.

10. Cut two strips bug print 2" x 32"; sew a strip to opposite long sides of pieced center. Press seams toward strips.

11. Cut two strips bug print 2" x 26"; sew to top and bottom of pieced center. Press seams toward strips.

12. Cut two strips blue print 4½" x 35"; sew a strip to opposite long sides of pieced center. Press seams toward strips.

13. Cut two strips blue print 4½" x 34"; sew to top and bottom of pieced center. Press seams toward strips.

14. Sandwich batting between completed top and prepared backing. Pin or baste layers together to hold flat.

15. Machine-quilt in the ditch of seams or as desired. When quilting is complete, remove pins or basting, clip threads and trim edges even.

16. Bind edges with self-made or purchased binding to finish. ❖

# Seminole Crayons

BY KAREN NEARY

Kids love crayons, but sometimes the love messages created by those crayons are left in places you'd just as soon not discover. These crayons, however, won't leave any love letters on your walls! Using the Seminole piecing method, these crayons become a quilt before anyone has time to leave messages—except your message of love.

## Project Specifications
Quilt Size: 44" x 52"

## Fabric & Batting
- ¼ yard white-on-white print
- ¼ yard each green, brown and orange solids
- ½ yard each red, blue, yellow and purple solids
- ½ yard black solid
- 1½ yards cream-on-cream print
- Backing 47" x 57"
- Quilter's fleece 47" x 57"
- 6 yards self-made or purchased binding

## Supplies & Tools
- Neutral color all-purpose thread
- Black embroidery thread
- Invisible clear quilting thread
- ½ yard fusible transfer web
- ½ yard tear-off fabric stabilizer
- Basic sewing tools and supplies, rotary cutter, mat and ruler

## Instructions

### Making Crayon Points
1. Cut one 3" by fabric width strip from each of the seven solids and white-on-white print. Cut eight 4" by fabric width strips cream-on-cream print.

2. Sew a cream-on-cream print strip to each colored strip with right sides together along length; press seams toward darker fabrics.

3. Fold each strip in half with right sides together, aligning seams. Cut 2½" segments at a 45-degree angle as shown in Figure 1.

Seminole Crayons

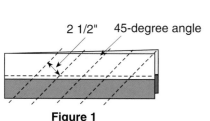

2 1/2"   45-degree angle

**Figure 1**
Fold each strip in half with right sides together, aligning seams. Cut 2 1/2" segments at a 45-degree angle as shown.

**Figure 2**
Join 2 same-color segments, using 1 of each angle.

4. Join two same-color segments, using one of each angle as shown in Figure 2.

5. Join stitched units in the following color order referring to Figure 3; yellow, blue, brown, red, white, green, orange and purple. Press seams in one direction.

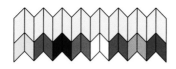

**Figure 3**
Join units in the color order shown.

6. Trim strip across top and bottom ¼" past the seam line on the colored end and 3¼" past the top colored point on the cream end as shown in Figure 4; set aside. The strip should measure 5½" x 32½". Repeat for two strips.

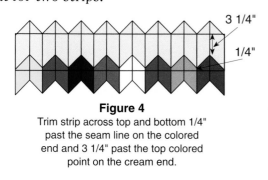

3 1/4"

1/4"

**Figure 4**
Trim strip across top and bottom 1/4" past the seam line on the colored end and 3 1/4" past the top colored point on the cream end.

### Making Crayon Body Sections

1. Cut one strip of each color and white-on-white print 4½" by fabric width. Sew together along length in the same order as in step 5; press seams in one direction.

2. Cut two 14½" body sections and two 2" bottom sections from the pieced strip set as shown in Figure 5.

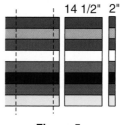

14 1/2"   2"

**Figure 5**
Cut two 14 1/2" body sections and two 2" bottom sections from the pieced strip set.

3. Cut four strips black solid 1" x 32½". Sew a black solid strip to the top and bottom of one body section; sew a bottom section to the bottom and a point section to the top as shown in Figure 6. Press seams toward black solid. Repeat for two pieced sections.

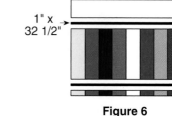

1" x 32 1/2"

**Figure 6**
Sew a black solid strip to the top and bottom of 1 body section; sew a bottom section to the bottom and a point section to the top as shown.

# Seminole Crayons

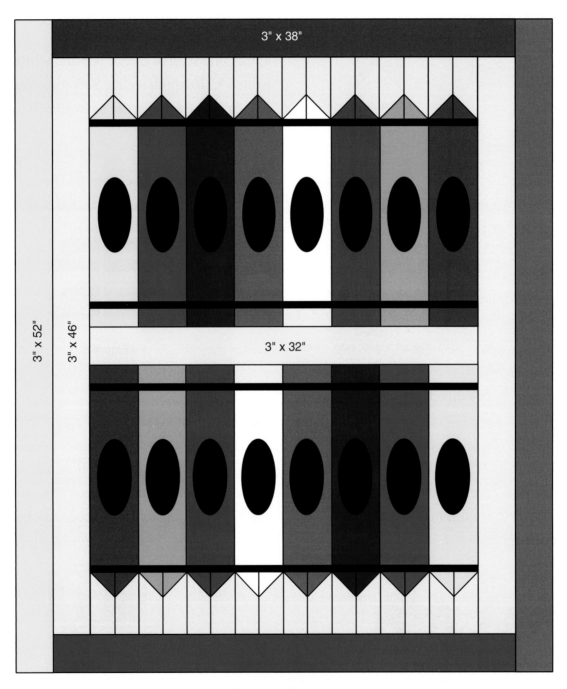

3" x 52"

3" x 46"

3" x 38"

3" x 32"

**Seminole Crayons**
Placement Diagram
44" x 52"

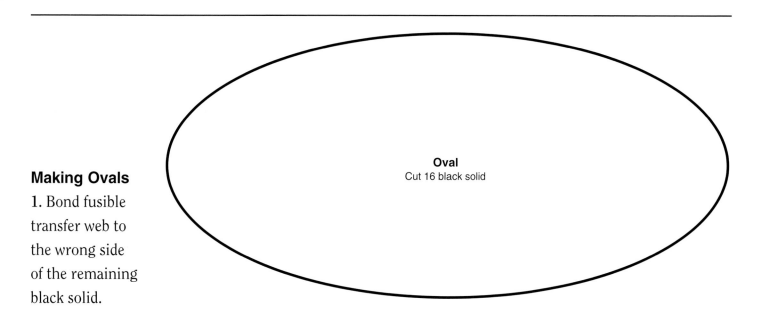

**Oval**
Cut 16 black solid

## Making Ovals

1. Bond fusible transfer web to the wrong side of the remaining black solid.

2. Prepare template for oval using pattern given; trace onto the paper side of the fused black solid as directed on pattern for number to cut. Cut out shapes on traced line; remove paper backing.

3. Center and fuse an oval on each body section of each crayon. Place tear-off fabric stabilizer behind each fused shape and machine-appliqué in place using black embroidery thread. When stitching is complete, remove fabric stabilizer.

## Assembling Top

1. Cut one strip cream-on-cream print 3½" x 32½". Join the two pieced sections with the strip referring to the Placement Diagram for positioning of strips; press seams away from pieced strip sections.

2. Cut and piece two strips cream-on-cream print 3½" x 46½. Sew a strip to opposite long sides of the pieced center.

3. Cut one strip each purple and blue solids 3½" x 38½"; sew a strip to the top and bottom of the pieced center referring to the Placement Diagram for positioning of colors. Press seams toward strips.

4. Cut and piece one strip each yellow and red solids 3½" x 52½". Sew a strip to opposite long sides of the pieced center referring to the Placement Diagram for positioning of colors; press seams toward strips.

5. Sandwich batting between completed top and prepared backing; pin or baste to hold.

6. Quilt as desired by hand or machine. *Note: The quilt shown was machine-quilted in a diagonal grid using invisible clear quilting thread in the top of the machine and all-purpose thread in the bobbin.*

7. Remove pins or basting. Trim edges even with quilted top. Bind edges with self-made or purchased binding to finish. ❖

# Little Blue Shoes

BY MILLIE EMERSON

This Sunbonnet Sue quilt was inspired by the poem of the same name from *Marigold Garden* by Kate Greenaway. Wouldn't it be the perfect quilt for a sweet little girl?

> *Little Blue Shoes mustn't go*
> *Very far alone, you know,*
> *Else she'll fall down*
> *Or, lose her way,*
> *Fancy—what*
> *Would mamma say?*
> *Better put her little hand*
> *Under sister's wise command,*
> *When she's a little older grown*
> *Blue Shoes may go alone.*
>
> —Kate Greenaway

# Little Blue Shoes

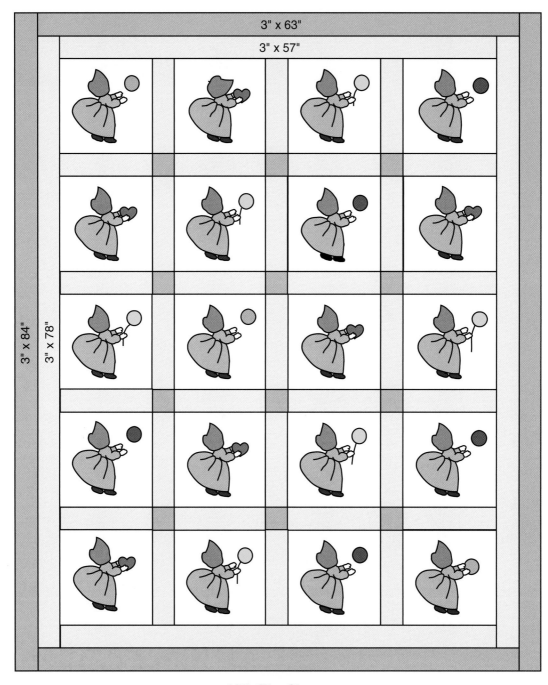

**Little Blue Shoes**
Placement Diagram
69" x 84"

# Little Blue Shoes

## Project Specifications

Quilt Size: 69" x 84"

Block Size: 12" x 12"

Number of Blocks: 20

## Fabric & Batting

- ¼ yard dark pink solid
- Scraps blue and yellow
- 8" x 9" piece red solid
- 2 yards light pink solid
- 2⅛ yards pastel plaid
- 2½ yards white solid
- Backing 73" x 88"
- Batting 73" x 88"
- 9 yards self-made or purchased binding

## Supplies & Tools

- Black all-purpose thread
- White quilting thread
- 3½ yards fusible transfer web
- 3½ yards tear-off fabric stabilizer
- Basic sewing tools and supplies

## Instructions

1. Prepare templates for each appliqué shape using full-size patterns given.

**Little Blue Shoes**
12" x 12" Block

2. Reverse and trace shapes on paper side of fusible transfer web referring to pattern for number to cut. Cut out shapes leaving a margin beyond traced lines.

3. Fuse shapes to fabrics as directed on patterns for color. Cut out shapes on traced lines; remove paper backing.

4. Cut 20 squares white solid 12½" x 12½". Fold and crease to mark centers on each block.

5. Arrange one design motif on each white solid square in numerical order, matching X marked on pattern with center creases; fuse in place. *Note: Hearts are held in six blocks and balloons or balls are held in 14 blocks. Refer to the Placement Diagram for arrangement of blocks.*

6. Cut tear-off fabric stabilizer to fit behind each design motif; pin in place.

# Little Blue Shoes

7. Using black all-purpose thread in the top of the machine and in the bobbin, machine-appliqué shapes in place. Zigzag-stitch detail lines and hand shapes. Remove tear-off stabilizer.

8. Cut three strips light pink solid 12½" by fabric width. Cut each strip into 3½" segments for sashing strips. You will need 31 strips.

9. Cut one strip pastel plaid 3½" by fabric width. Cut strip into 3½" segments for sashing squares; you will need 12 sashing squares.

10. Join three appliquéd blocks with three 3½" x 12½" sashing strips to make a block row as shown in Figure 1; press seams toward strips. Repeat for five rows.

**Figure 1**
Join 4 blocks with 3 sashing strips to make a block row.

11. Join four 3½" x 12½" sashing strips with three 3½" x 3½" sashing squares to make a sashing row; press seams toward strips. Repeat for four sashing rows.

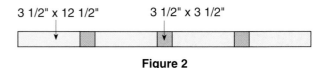

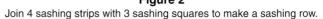

**Figure 2**
Join 4 sashing strips with 3 sashing squares to make a sashing row.

12. Join block rows with sashing rows referring to the Placement Diagram for positioning of rows; press seams in one direction.

13. Cut and piece two strips each light pink solid 3½" x 78½" and 3½" x 57½". Sew the longer strips to opposite long sides and shorter strips to top and bottom of pieced center; press seams toward strips.

14. Cut and piece two strips each pastel plaid 3½" x 84½" and 3½" x 63½". Sew the longer strips to the opposite long sides and shorter strips to top and bottom of pieced center; press seams toward strips.

15. Sandwich batting between completed top and prepared backing piece; pin or baste layers together to hold.

16. Quilt as desired by hand or machine. When quilting is complete, trim edges even; bind with self-made or purchased binding to finish. ❖

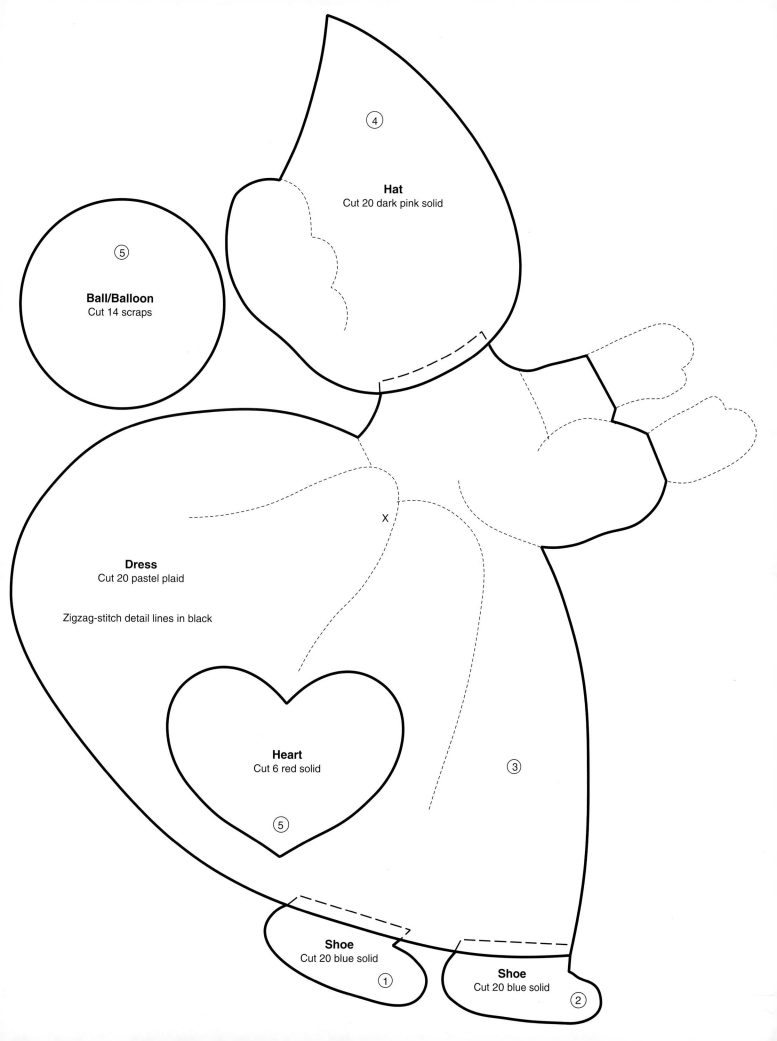

**Hat**
Cut 20 dark pink solid

④

⑤

**Ball/Balloon**
Cut 14 scraps

**Dress**
Cut 20 pastel plaid

Zigzag-stitch detail lines in black

X

**Heart**
Cut 6 red solid

⑤

③

**Shoe**
Cut 20 blue solid

①

**Shoe**
Cut 20 blue solid

②

# Love & Kisses

BY LINDA DENNER

Fat-eighth pastel prints are used to make the hearts in this quilt, but you can make these 18 hearts from the same fabric or fabric from your personal fabric stash. The kisses in this quilt are provided by the hearts. The love is provided by you as you make this quilt for a special baby.

# Love & Kisses

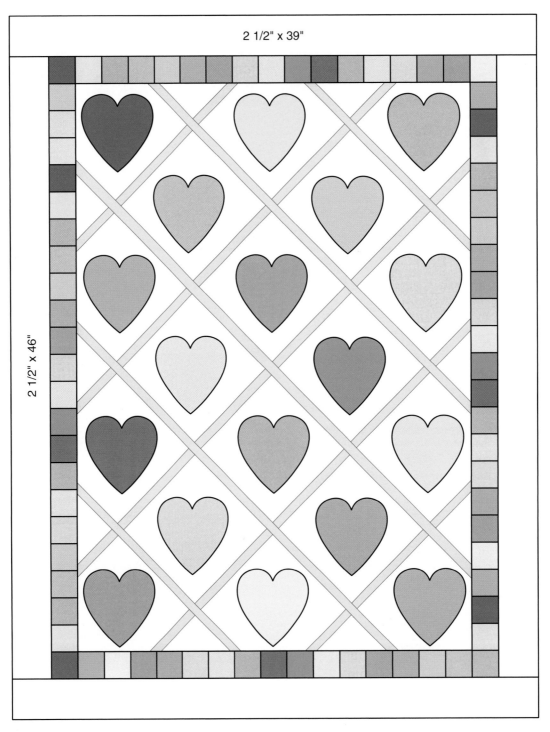

2 1/2" x 39"

2 1/2" x 46"

**Love & Kisses**
Placement Diagram
39" x 51"

# Love & Kisses

## Project Specifications
Quilt Size: 39" x 51"

## Fabric & Batting
- 18 fat eighths pastel prints
- 1⅝ yards white solid
- Backing 43" x 55"
- Batting 43" x 55"
- 5½ yards self-made or purchased binding

## Supplies & Tools
- Black and white all-purpose thread
- 1¼ yards fusible transfer web
- 1¼ yards fabric stabilizer
- 8½ yards yellow-check ⅝"-wide ribbon
- 8½ yards ¼"-wide fusible transfer web tape
- Basic sewing tools and supplies, rotary cutter, mat and ruler, yardstick, masking tape and water-erasable marker or pencil

## Instructions
1. Cut a 31" x 43" rectangle white solid for background and two strips each 3" x 46½" and 3" x 39½" for outside border strips.

2. Tape the background rectangle to a flat surface; draw a 30" x 42" rectangle on the piece using the water-erasable marker or pencil and the yardstick.

Mark a 6" grid within the marked box as shown in Figure 1.

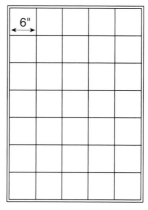
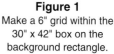

**Figure 1**
Make a 6" grid within the
30" x 42" box on the
background rectangle.

3. Referring to Figure 2, draw diagonal lines on the grid using the water-erasable marker or pencil.
*Note: These lines are used as guides for stitching on the yellow-check ⅝"-wide ribbon.*

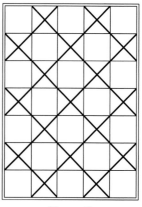

**Figure 2**
Draw diagonal lines
on the grid as shown.

# Love & Kisses

4. Prepare template for heart shape using pattern given. Trace heart shape onto the wrong side of the fusible transfer web; cut out shapes leaving a margin around each one.

5. Fuse one heart shape to the wrong side of each pastel print following manufacturer's instructions.

6. Cut out heart shapes on traced lines; remove paper backing.

7. Center a heart shape in each box created by the diagonal lines on the drawn grid; fuse in place.

8. Cut 18 squares fabric stabilizer 7" x 7". Pin one square behind each heart shape.

9. Using black all-purpose thread and a machine buttonhole or other decorative stitch, sew around outside edges of each heart shape; remove fabric stabilizer.

10. Bond ¼"-wide fusible transfer web to each diagonal line on the background fabric; remove paper backing.

11. Center and fuse the ⅝"-wide yellow-check ribbon to the fusible transfer web tape, covering each line and referring to Figure 3 for order of placement.

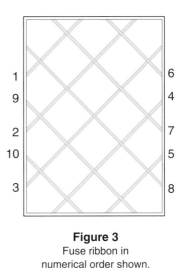

**Figure 3**
Fuse ribbon in
numerical order shown.

12. Stitch the ribbon in place on both sides of ribbon as in step 9.

13. Trim the background piece to 30½" x 42½".

14. Cut 76 squares pastel prints 2½" x 2½" for pieced border strips.

15. Join 15 pastel print squares to make a strip; repeat for two strips. Press seams in one direction. Repeat for two strips with 23 squares.

16. Sew the shorter strips to the top and bottom and longer strips to opposite long sides; press seams toward strips.

17. Sew longer white solid border strips cut in step 1 to opposite long sides of center and shorter strips to the top and bottom; press seams toward strips.

**18.** Sandwich batting between prepared backing and pieced top; pin or baste to hold.

**19.** Hand- or machine-quilt as desired. *Note: The sample shown was machine-quilted ¼" from each heart shape and in ditch of seams using white thread.*

**20.** Trim backing and batting even with top; remove pins or basting.

**21.** Bind with self-made or purchased binding to finish. ❖

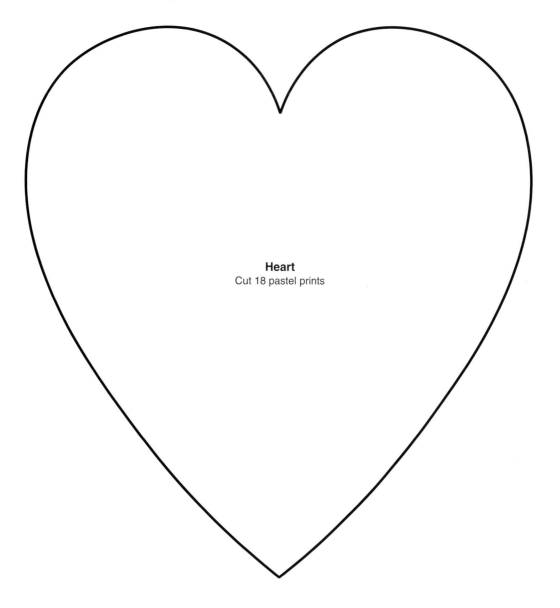

**Heart**
Cut 18 pastel prints

# General Instructions

## Quiltmaking Basics

### Materials & Supplies

#### Fabrics

**Fabric Choices.** Quilts and quilted projects combine fabrics of many types. Use same-fiber-content fabrics when making quilted items, if possible.

**Buying Fabrics.** One hundred percent cotton fabrics are recommended for making quilts. Choose colors similar to those used in the quilts shown or colors of your own preference. Most quilt designs depend more on contrast of values than on the colors used to create the design.

**Preparing the Fabric for Use.** Fabrics may be prewashed depending on your preference. Whether you prewash or not, be sure your fabrics are colorfast and won't run onto each other when washed after use.

**Fabric Grain.** Fabrics are woven with threads going in a crosswise and lengthwise direction. The threads cross at right angles—the more threads per inch, the stronger the fabric.

The crosswise threads will stretch a little. The lengthwise threads will not stretch at all. Cutting the fabric at a 45-degree angle to the crosswise and lengthwise threads produces a bias edge which stretches a great deal when pulled (Figure 1).

If templates are given with patterns in this book, pay careful attention to the grain lines marked with arrows. These arrows indicate that the piece should be placed on the lengthwise grain with the arrow running on one thread. Although it is not necessary to examine the fabric and find a thread to match to, it is important to try to place the arrow with the lengthwise grain of the fabric (Figure 2).

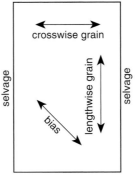

**Figure 1**
Drawing shows lengthwise, crosswise and bias threads.

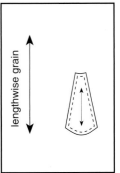

**Figure 2**
Place the template with marked arrow on the lengthwise grain of the fabric.

### Thread

For most piecing, good-quality cotton or cotton-covered polyester is the thread of choice. Inexpensive polyester threads are not recommended because they can cut the fibers of cotton fabrics.

Choose a color thread that will match or blend with the fabrics in your quilt. For projects pieced with dark and light color fabrics choose a neutral thread color, such as a medium gray, as a compromise between colors. Test by pulling a sample seam.

### Batting

Batting is the material used to give a quilt loft or thickness. It also adds warmth.

Batting size is listed in inches for each pattern to reflect the size needed to complete the quilt according to the instructions. Purchase the size large enough to cut the size you need for the quilt of your choice.

Some qualities to look for in batting are drapability, resistance to fiber migration, loft and softness.

## Tools & Equipment

There are few truly essential tools and little equipment required for quiltmaking. Basics include needles (hand-sewing and quilting betweens), pins (long, thin, sharp pins are best), sharp scissors or shears, a thimble, template materials (plastic or cardboard), marking tools (chalk marker, water-erasable pen and a No. 2 pencil are a few) and a quilting frame or hoop. For piecing and/or quilting by machine, add a sewing machine to the list.

Other sewing basics such as a seam ripper, pincushion, measuring tape and an iron are also necessary. For choosing colors or quilting designs for your quilt, or for designing your own quilt, it is helpful to have on hand graph paper, tracing paper, colored pencils or markers and a ruler.

For making strip-pieced quilts, a rotary cutter, mat and specialty rulers are often used. We recommend an ergonomic rotary cutter, a large self-healing mat and several rulers. If you can choose only one size, a 6" x 24" marked in ⅛" or ¼" increments is recommended.

## Construction Methods

**Traditional Templates.** While some quilt instructions in this book use rotary-cut strips and quick sewing methods, many patterns require a template. Templates are like the pattern pieces used to sew a garment. They are used to cut the fabric pieces that make up the quilt top. There are two types—templates that include a ¼" seam allowance and those that don't.

Choose the template material and the pattern. Transfer the pattern shapes to the template material with a sharp No. 2 lead pencil. Write the pattern name, piece letter or number, grain line and number to cut for one block or whole quilt on each piece as shown in Figure 3.

Some patterns require a reversed piece (Figure 4). These patterns are labeled with an R after the piece letter; for example, B and BR. To reverse a template, first cut it with the labeled side up and then with the labeled side down. Compare these to the right and left fronts of a blouse. When making a garment, you accomplish reversed pieces when cutting the pattern on two

layers of fabric placed with right sides together. This can be done when cutting templates as well.

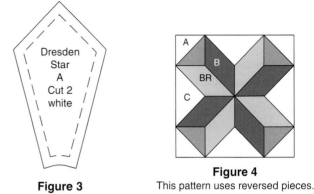

**Figure 3**
Mark each template with the pattern name and piece identification.

**Figure 4**
This pattern uses reversed pieces.

If cutting one layer of fabric at a time, first trace the template onto the backside of the fabric with the marked side down; turn the template over with the marked side up to make reverse pieces.

**Hand-Piecing Basics.** When hand-piecing it is easier to begin with templates that do not include the ¼" seam allowance. Place the template on the wrong side of the fabric, lining up the marked grain line with lengthwise or crosswise fabric grain. If the piece does not have to be reversed, place with labeled side up. Trace around shape; move, leaving ½" between the shapes, and mark again.

When you have marked the appropriate number of pieces, cut out pieces, leaving ¼" beyond marked line all around each piece.

To join two units, place the patches with right sides together. Stick a pin in at the beginning of the seam through both fabric patches, matching the beginning points (Figure 5); for hand-piecing, the seam begins on the traced line, not at the edge of the fabric (see Figure 6).

**Figure 5**
Stick a pin through fabrics to match the beginning of the seam.

**Figure 6**
Begin hand-piecing at seam, not at the edge of the fabric. Continue stitching along seam line.

# General Instructions

Thread a sharp needle; knot one strand of the thread at the end. Remove the pin and insert the needle in the hole; make a short stitch and then a backstitch right over the first stitch. Continue making short stitches with several stitches on the needle at one

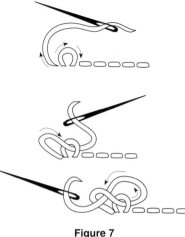

**Figure 7**
Make a loop in backstitch to make a knot.

time. As you stitch, check the back piece often to assure accurate stitching on the seam line. Take a stitch at the end of the seam; backstitch and knot at the same time as shown in Figure 7. Seams on hand-pieced fabric patches may be finger-pressed toward the darker fabric.

To sew units together, pin fabric patches together, matching seams. Sew as above except where seams meet; at these intersections, backstitch, go through seam to next piece and backstitch again to secure seam joint.

Not all pieced blocks can be stitched with straight seams or in rows. Some patterns require set-in pieces. To begin a set-in seam, pin one side of the square to the proper side of the star point with right sides together, matching corners. Start stitching at the seam line on the outside point; stitch on the marked seam line to the end of the seam line at the center referring to Figure 8.

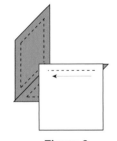

**Figure 8**
To set a square into a diamond point, match seams and stitch from outside edge to center.

Bring around the adjacent side and pin to the next star point, matching seams. Continue the stitching line from the adjacent seam through corners and to the outside edge of the square as shown in Figure 9.

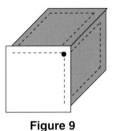

**Figure 9**
Continue stitching the adjacent side of the square to the next diamond shape in 1 seam from center to outside as shown.

**Machine-Piecing.** If making templates, include the ¼" seam allowance on the template for machine-piecing. Place template on the wrong side of the fabric as for hand-piecing except butt pieces against one another when tracing.

Set machine on 2.5 or 12–15 stitches per inch. Join pieces as for hand-piecing for set-in seams; but for other straight seams, begin and end sewing at the end of the fabric patch sewn as shown in Figure 10. No backstitching is necessary when machine-stitching.

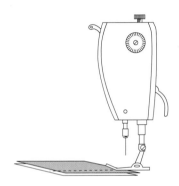

**Figure 10**
Begin machine-piecing at the end of the piece, not at the end of the seam.

Join units as for hand-piecing referring to the piecing diagrams where needed. Chain piecing (Figure 11—sewing several like units before sewing other units) saves time by eliminating beginning and ending stitches.

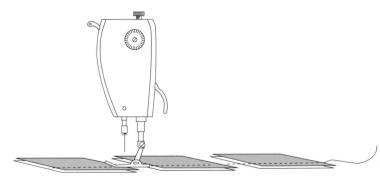

**Figure 11**
Units may be chain-pieced to save time.

When joining machine-pieced units, match seams against each other with seam allowances pressed in opposite directions to reduce bulk and make perfect matching of seams possible (Figure 12).

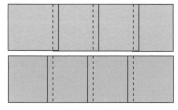

**Figure 12**
Sew machine-pieced units with seams
pressed in opposite directions.

**Quick-Cutting.** Templates can be completely eliminated when using a rotary cutter with a plastic ruler and mat to cut fabric strips.

When rotary-cutting strips, straighten raw edges of fabric by folding fabric in fourths across the width as shown in Figure 13. Press down flat; place ruler on fabric square with edge of fabric and make one cut from the folded edge to the outside edge. If strips are not straightened, a wavy strip will result as shown in Figure 14.

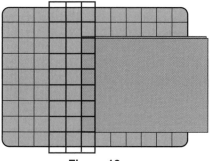

**Figure 13**
Fold fabric and straighten as shown.

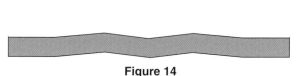

**Figure 14**
Wavy strips result if fabric is not straightened before cutting.

Always cut away from your body, holding the ruler firmly with the non-cutting hand. Keep fingers away from the edge of the ruler as it is easy for the rotary cutter to slip and jump over the edge of the ruler if cutting is not properly done.

If a square is required for the pattern, it can be subcut from a strip as shown in Figure 15.

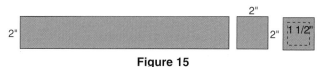

**Figure 15**
If cutting squares, cut proper-width strip into same-width segments.
Here, a 2" strip is cut into 2" segments to create 2" squares. These
squares finish at 1 1/2" when sewn.

If you need right triangles with the straight grain on the short sides, you can use the same method, but you need to figure out how wide to cut the strip. Measure the finished size of one short side of the triangle. Add ⅞" to this size for seam allowance. Cut fabric strips this width; cut the strips into the same increment to create squares. Cut the squares on the diagonal to produce triangles. For example, if you need a triangle with a 2" finished height, cut the strips 2⅞" by the width of the fabric. Cut the strips into 2⅞" squares. Cut each square on the diagonal to produce the correct-size triangle with the grain on the short sides (Figure 16).

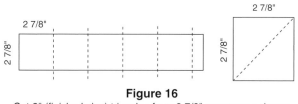

**Figure 16**
Cut 2" (finished size) triangles from 2 7/8" squares as shown.

Triangles sewn together to make squares are called half-square triangles or triangle/squares. When joined, the triangle/square unit has the straight of grain on all outside edges of the block.

Another method of making triangle/squares is shown in Figure 17. Layer two squares with right sides together; draw a diagonal line through the center. Stitch ¼" on both sides of the line.

# General Instructions

Cut apart on the drawn line to reveal two stitched triangle/squares.

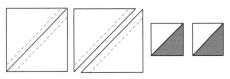

**Figure 17**
Mark a diagonal line on the square; stitch
1/4" on each side of the line. Cut on line
to reveal stitched triangle/squares.

If you need triangles with the straight of grain on the diagonal, such as for fill-in triangles on the outside edges of a diagonal-set quilt, the procedure is a bit different.

To make these triangles, a square is cut on both diagonals; thus, the straight of grain is on the longest or diagonal side (Figure 18). To figure out the size to cut the square, add 1¼" to the needed finished size of the longest side of the triangle. For example, if you need a triangle with a 12" finished diagonal, cut a 13¼" square.

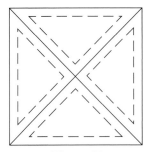

**Figure 18**
Add 1 1/4" to the finished size of the
longest side of the triangle needed
and cut on both diagonals to make a
quarter-square triangle.

If templates are given, use their measurments to cut fabric strips to correspond with that measurement. The template may be used on the strip to cut pieces quickly. Strip cutting works best for squares, triangles, rectangles and diamonds. Odd-shaped templates are difficult to cut in multiple layers or using a rotary cutter.

**Quick-Piecing Method.**
Lay pieces to be joined under the presser foot of the sewing machine right sides together. Sew an exact ¼" seam allowance to the end of the piece; place another unit right next to the first one and continue sewing, adding a piece after every stitched piece, until all of the pieces are used up (Figure 19).

**Figure 19**
Sew pieces together in a chain.

When sewing is finished, cut threads joining the pieces apart. Press seam toward the darker fabric.

## Appliqué

**Appliqué.** Appliqué is the process of applying one piece of fabric on top of another for decorative or functional purposes.

**Making Templates.** Most appliqué designs given here are shown as full-size drawings for the completed designs. The drawings show dotted lines to indicate where one piece overlaps another. Other marks indicate placement of embroidery stitches for decorative purposes such as eyes, lips, flowers, etc.

For hand appliqué, trace each template onto the right side of the fabric with template right side up. Cut around shape, adding a ⅛"–1¼" seam allowance.

Before the actual appliqué process begins, cut the background block. If you have a full-size drawing of the design, it might help you to draw on the background block to help with placement.

Transfer the design to a large piece of tracing paper. Place the paper on top of the design; use masking tape to hold in place. Trace design onto paper.

If you don't have a light box, tape the pattern on a window; center the background block on top and tape in place. Trace the design onto the background block with a water-erasable marker or light lead or chalk pencil. This drawing will mark exactly where the fabric pieces should be placed on the background block.

**Hand Appliqué.** Traditional hand appliqué uses a template made from the desired finished shape without seam allowance added.

After fabric is prepared, trace the desired shape onto the right side of the fabric with a water-erasable marker or light lead or chalk pencil. Leave at least ½" between design motifs when tracing to allow for the seam allowance when cutting out the shapes.

When the desired number of shapes needed has been drawn on the fabric pieces, cut out shapes leaving ⅛"–¼" all around drawn line for turning under.

Turn the shape's edges over on the drawn or stitched line. When turning in concave curves, clip to seams and baste the seam allowance over as shown in Figure 20.

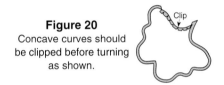

**Figure 20**
Concave curves should
be clipped before turning
as shown.

During the actual appliqué process, you may be layering one shape on top of another. Where two fabrics overlap, the underneath piece does not have to be turned under or stitched down.

If possible, trim away the underneath fabric when the block is finished by carefully cutting away the background from underneath and then cutting away unnecessary layers to reduce bulk and avoid shadows from darker fabrics showing through on light fabrics.

For hand appliqué, position the fabric shapes on the background block and pin or baste them in place. Using a blind stitch or appliqué stitch, sew pieces in place with matching thread and small stitches. Start with background pieces first and work up to foreground pieces. Appliqué the pieces in place on the background in numerical order, if given, layering as necessary.

**Machine Appliqué.** There are several products available to help make the machine-appliqué process easier and faster.

Fusible transfer web is a commercial product similar to iron-on interfacings except it has two sticky sides. It is used to adhere appliqué shapes to the background with heat. Paper is adhered to one side of the web.

To use, reverse pattern and draw shapes onto the paper side of the web; cut, leaving a margin around each shape. Place on the wrong side of the chosen fabric; fuse in place referring to the manufacturer's instructions. Cut out shapes on the drawn line. Peel off the paper and fuse in place on the background fabric. Transfer any detail lines to the fabric shapes. This process adds a little bulk or stiffness to the appliquéd shape and makes hand-quilting through the layers difficult.

For successful machine appliqué a tear-off stabilizer is recommended. This product is placed under the background fabric while machine appliqué is being done. It is torn away when the work is finished. This kind of stabilizer keeps the background fabric from pulling during the machine-appliqué process.

During the actual machine-appliqué process, you will be layering one shape on top of another. Where two fabrics overlap, the underneath piece does not have to be turned under or stitched down.

Thread the top of the machine with thread to match the fabric patches or with threads that coordinate or contrast with fabrics. Rayon thread is a good choice when a sheen is desired on the finished appliqué stitches. Do not use rayon thread in the bobbin; use all-purpose thread.

When all machine work is complete, remove stabilizer from the back referring to the manufacturer's instructions.

# Putting It All Together

## Finishing the Top

**Settings.** Most quilts are made by sewing individual blocks together in rows that, when joined, create a design. There are several other methods used to join blocks. Sometimes the setting choice is determined by the block's design. For example, a House block should be placed upright on a quilt, not sideways or upside down.

Plain blocks can be alternated with pieced or appliquéd blocks in a straight set. Making a quilt using plain blocks saves time;

# General Instructions

half the number of pieced or appliquéd blocks are needed to make the same-size quilt as shown in Figure 1.

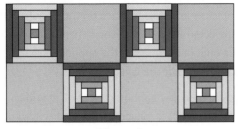

**Figure 1**
Alternate plain blocks with pieced blocks to save time.

**Adding Borders.** Borders are an integral part of the quilt and should complement the colors and designs used in the quilt center. Borders frame a quilt just like a mat and frame do a picture.

If fabric strips are added for borders, they may be mitered or butted at the corners as shown in Figures 2 and 3. To determine the size for butted border strips, measure across the center of the completed quilt top from one side raw edge to the other side raw edge. This measurement will include a ¼" seam allowance.

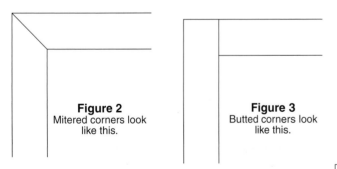

**Figure 2**
Mitered corners look like this.

**Figure 3**
Butted corners look like this.

Cut two border strips that length by the chosen width of the border. Sew these strips to the top and bottom of the pieced center referring to Figure 4. Press the seam allowance toward the border strips.

Measure across the completed quilt top at the center, from top raw edge to bottom raw edge, including the two border strips

already added. Cut two border strips that length by the chosen width of the border. Sew a strip to each of the two remaining sides as shown in Figure 4. Press the seams toward the border strips.

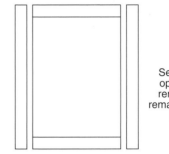

**Figure 4**
Sew border strips to opposite sides; sew remaining 2 strips to remaining sides to make butted corners.

To make mitered corners, measure the quilt as before. To this add twice the width of the border and ½" for seam allowances to determine the length of the strips. Repeat for opposite sides. Sew on each strip, stopping stitching ¼" from corner, leaving the remainder of the strip dangling.

Press corners at a 45-degree angle to form a crease. Stitch from the inside quilt corner to the outside on the creased line. Trim excess away after stitching and press mitered seams open (Figures 5–7).

Carefully press the entire piece, including the pieced center. Avoid pulling and stretching while pressing, which would distort shapes.

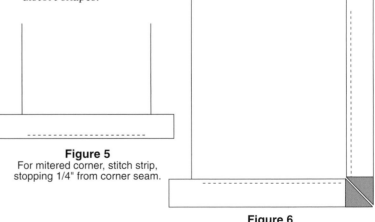

**Figure 5**
For mitered corner, stitch strip, stopping 1/4" from corner seam.

**Figure 6**
Fold and press corner to make a 45-degree angle.

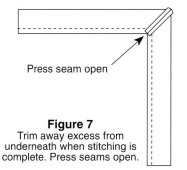

**Figure 7**
Trim away excess from underneath when stitching is complete. Press seams open.

Press seam open

## Getting Ready to Quilt

**Choosing a Quilting Design.** If you choose to hand- or machine-quilt your finished top, you will need to select a design for quilting.

There are several types of quilting designs, some of which may not have to be marked. The easiest of the unmarked designs is in-the-ditch quilting. Here the quilting stitches are placed in the valley created by the seams joining two pieces together or next to the edge of an appliqué design. There is no need to mark a top for in-the-ditch quilting. Machine quilters choose this option because the stitches are not as obvious on the finished quilt. (Figure 8).

Outline-quilting ¼" or more away from seams or appliqué shapes is another no-mark alternative (Figure 9) that prevents having to sew through the layers made by seams, thus making stitching easier.

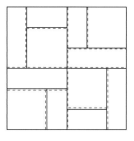

**Figure 8**
In-the-ditch quilting is done in the seam that joins 2 pieces.

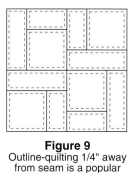

**Figure 9**
Outline-quilting 1/4" away from seam is a popular choice for quilting.

If you are not comfortable eyeballing the ¼" (or other distance), masking tape is available in different widths and is helpful to place on straight-edge designs to mark the quilting line. If using masking tape, place the tape right up against the seam and quilt close to the other edge.

**Figure 10**
Machine meander quilting fills in large spaces.

Meander or free-motion quilting by machine fills in open spaces and doesn't require marking. It is fun and easy to stitch as shown in Figure 10.

**Marking the Top for Quilting.** If you choose a fancy or allover design for quilting, you will need to transfer the design to your quilt top before layering with the backing and batting. You may use a sharp medium-lead or silver pencil on light background fabrics. Test the pencil marks to guarantee that they will wash out of your quilt top when quilting is complete; or be sure your quilting stitches cover the pencil marks. Mechanical pencils with very fine points may be used successfully to mark quilts.

Manufactured quilt-design templates are available in many designs and sizes and are cut out of a durable plastic template material that is easy to use.

To make a permanent quilt-design template, choose a template material on which to transfer the design. See-through plastic is the best as it will let you place the design while allowing you to see where it is in relation to your quilt design without moving it. Place the design on the quilt top where you want it and trace around it with your marking tool. Pick up the quilting template and place again; repeat marking.

No matter what marking method you use, remember—the marked lines should never show on the finished quilt. When the top is marked, it is ready for layering.

**Preparing the Quilt Backing.** The quilt backing is a very important feature of your quilt. The materials listed for each quilt in this book includes the size requirements for the backing, not the yardage needed. Exceptions to this are when the backing fabric is also used on the quilt top and yardage is given for that fabric.

A backing is generally cut at least 4" larger than the quilt top or 2" larger on all sides. For a 64" x 78" finished quilt, the backing would need to be at least 68" x 82".

To avoid having the seam across the center of the quilt

backing, cut or tear one of the right-length pieces in half and sew half to each side of the second piece as shown in Figure 11.

Quilts that need a backing more than 88" wide may be pieced in horizontal pieces as shown in Figure 12.

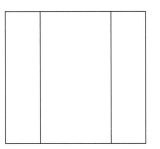

**Figure 11**
Center 1 backing piece with a piece on each side.

**Figure 12**
Horizontal seams may be used on backing pieces.

**Layering the Quilt Sandwich.** Layering the quilt top with the batting and backing is time-consuming. Open the batting several days before you need it and place over a bed or flat on the floor to help flatten the creases caused from its being folded up in the bag for so long.

Iron the backing piece, folding in half both vertically and horizontally and pressing to mark centers.

If you will not be quilting on a frame, place the backing right side down on a clean floor or table. Start in the center and push any wrinkles or bunches flat. Use masking tape to tape the edges to the floor or large clips to hold the backing to the

edges of the table. The backing should be taut.

Place the batting on top of the backing, matching centers using fold lines as guides; flatten out any wrinkles. Trim the batting to the same size as the backing.

Fold the quilt top in half lengthwise and place on top of the batting, wrong side against the batting, matching centers. Unfold quilt and, working from the center to the outside edges, smooth out any wrinkles or lumps.

To hold the quilt layers together for quilting, baste by hand or use safety pins. If basting by hand, thread a long thin needle with a long piece of unknotted white or off-white thread. Starting in the center and leaving a long tail, make 4"–6" stitches toward the outside edge of the quilt top, smoothing as you baste. Start at the center again and work toward the outside as shown in Figure 13.

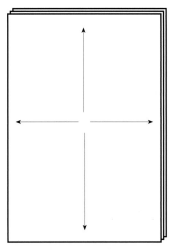

**Figure 13**
Baste from the center to the outside edges.

If quilting by machine, you may prefer to use safety pins for holding your fabric sandwich together. Start in the center of the quilt and pin to the outside, leaving pins open until all are placed. When you are satisfied that all layers are smooth, close the pins.

## Quilting
**Hand Quilting.** Hand quilting is the process of placing stitches through the quilt top, batting and backing to hold them

together. While it is a functional process, it also adds beauty and loft to the finished quilt.

To begin, thread a sharp between needle with an 18" piece of quilting thread. Tie a small knot in the end of the thread. Position the needle about ½" to 1" away from the starting point on quilt top. Sink the needle through the top into the batting layer but not through the backing. Pull the needle up at the starting point of the quilting design. Pull the needle and thread until the knot sinks through the top into the batting (Figure 14).

Some stitchers like to take a backstitch here at the beginning while others prefer to begin the first stitch here. Take small, even running stitches along the marked quilting line (Figure 15). Keep one hand positioned underneath to feel the needle go all the way through to the backing.

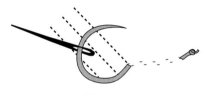

**Figure 14**
Start the needle through the top layer of fabric 1/2"–1"
away from quilting line with knot on top of fabric.

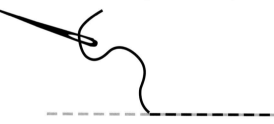

**Figure 15**
Make small, even running stitches on marked quilting line.

When you have nearly run out of thread, wind the thread around the needle several times to make a small knot and pull it close to the fabric. Insert the needle into the fabric on the quilting line and come out with the needle ½" to 1" away, pulling the knot into the fabric layers the same as when you started. Pull and cut thread close to fabric. The end should disappear inside after cutting. Some quilters prefer to take a backstitch with a loop through it for a knot to end.

**Machine Quilting.** Successful machine quilting requires practice and a good relationship with your sewing machine.

Prepare the quilt for machine quilting in the same way as for hand quilting. Use safety pins to hold the layers together instead of basting with thread.

Presser-foot quilting is best used for straight-line quilting because the presser bar lever does not need to be continually lifted.

Set the machine on a longer stitch length (3.0 or 8–10 stitches to the inch). Too tight a stitch causes puckering and fabric tucks, either on the quilt top or backing. An even-feed or walking foot helps to eliminate the tucks and puckering by feeding the upper and lower layers through the machine evenly. Before you begin, loosen the amount of pressure on the presser foot.

Special machine-quilting needles work best to penetrate the three layers in your quilt.

Decide on a design. Quilting in the ditch is not quite as visible, but if you quilt with the feed dogs engaged, it means turning the quilt frequently. It is not easy to fit a rolled-up quilt through the small opening on the sewing machine head.

Meander quilting is the easiest way to machine-quilt—and it is fun. Meander quilting is done using an appliqué or darning foot with the feed dogs dropped. It is sort of like scribbling. Simply move the quilt top around under the foot and make stitches in a random pattern to fill the space. The same method may be used to outline a quilt design. The trick is the same as in hand quilting; you are striving for stitches of uniform size. Your hands are in complete control of the design.

If machine quilting is of interest to you, there are several very good books available at quilt shops that will help you become a successful machine quilter.

## Finishing the Edges

After your quilt is tied or quilted, the edges need to be finished. Decide how you want the edges of your quilt finished before layering the backing and batting with the quilt top.

**Without Binding—Self-Finish.** There is one way to eliminate adding an edge finish. This is done before quilting. Place the batting on a flat surface. Place the pieced top right side up on the batting. Place the backing right sides together with the pieced top. Pin and/or baste the layers together to hold flat referring to Layering the Quilt Sandwich.

# General Instructions

Begin stitching in the center of one side using a ¼" seam allowance, reversing at the beginning and end of the seam. Continue stitching all around and back to the beginning side. Leave a 12" or larger opening. Clip corners to reduce excess. Turn right side out through the opening. Slipstitch the opening closed by hand. The quilt may now be quilted by hand or machine.

The disadvantage to this method is that once the edges are sewn in, any creases or wrinkles that might form during the quilting process cannot be flattened out. Tying is the preferred method for finishing a quilt constructed using this method.

Bringing the backing fabric to the front is another way to finish the quilt's edge without binding. To accomplish this, complete the quilt as for hand or machine quilting. Trim the batting only even with the front. Trim the backing 1" larger than the completed top all around.

Turn the backing edge in ½" and then turn over to the front along edge of batting. The folded edge may be machine-stitched close to the edge through all layers, or blind-stitched in place to finish.

The front may be turned to the back. If using this method, a wider front border is needed. The backing and batting are trimmed 1" smaller than the top and the top edge is turned under ½" and then turned to the back and stitched in place.

One more method of self-finish may be used. The top and backing may be stitched together by hand at the edge. To accomplish this, all quilting must be stopped ½" from the quilt-top edge. The top and backing of the quilt are trimmed even and the batting is trimmed to ¼"–½" smaller. The edges of the top and backing are turned in ¼"–½" and blind-stitched together at the very edge.

These methods do not require the use of extra fabric and save time in preparation of binding strips; they are not as durable as an added binding.

**Binding.** The technique of adding extra fabric at the edges of the quilt is called binding. The binding encloses the edges and adds an extra layer of fabric for durability.

To prepare the quilt for the addition of the binding, trim the batting and backing layers flush with the top of the quilt using a rotary cutter and ruler or shears. Using a walking-foot attachment (sometimes called an even-feed foot attachment), machine-baste the three layers together all around approximately ⅛" from the cut edge.

The materials listed for each quilt in this book often includes a number of yards of self-made or purchased binding. Bias binding may be purchased in packages and in many colors. The advantage to self-made binding is that you can use fabrics from your quilt to coordinate colors. Double-fold, straight-grain binding and double-fold, bias-grain binding are two of the most commonly used types of binding.

Double-fold, straight-grain binding is used on smaller projects with right-angle corners. Double-fold, bias-grain binding is best suited for bed-size quilts or quilts with rounded corners.

To make double-fold, straight-grain binding, cut 2¼"-wide strips of fabric across the width or down the length of the fabric totaling the perimeter of the quilt plus 10". The strips are joined as shown in Figure 16 and pressed in half wrong sides together along the length using an iron on a cotton setting with no steam.

**Figure 16**
Join binding strips in a
diagonal seam to eliminate
bulk as shown.

Lining up the raw edges, place the binding on the top of the quilt and begin sewing (again using the walking foot) approximately 6" from the beginning of the binding strip. Stop sewing ¼" from the first corner, leave the needle in the quilt, turn and sew diagonally to the corner as shown in Figure 17.

Fold the binding at a 45-degree angle up and away from the quilt as shown in Figure 18 and back down flush with the raw edges. Starting at the top raw edge of the quilt, begin sewing the next side as shown in Figure 19. Repeat at the next three corners.

As you approach the beginning of the binding strip, stop stitching and overlap the binding ½" from the edge; trim. Join the two ends with a ¼" seam allowance and press the seam open. Reposition the joined binding along the edge of the quilt and resume stitching to the beginning.

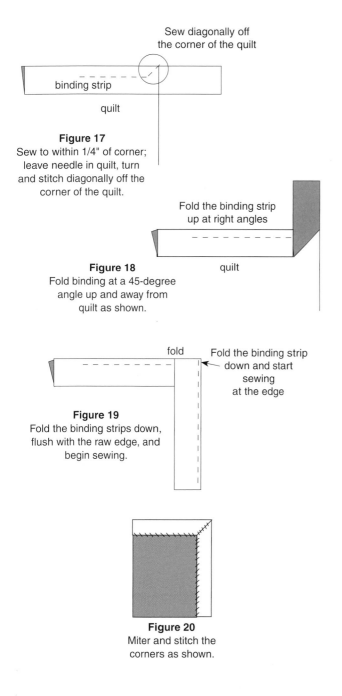

Sew diagonally off
the corner of the quilt

binding strip

quilt

**Figure 17**
Sew to within 1/4" of corner;
leave needle in quilt, turn
and stitch diagonally off the
corner of the quilt.

Fold the binding strip
up at right angles

quilt

**Figure 18**
Fold binding at a 45-degree
angle up and away from
quilt as shown.

fold

Fold the binding strip
down and start
sewing
at the edge

**Figure 19**
Fold the binding strips down,
flush with the raw edge, and
begin sewing.

**Figure 20**
Miter and stitch the
corners as shown.

To finish, bring the folded edge of the binding over the raw edges and blind-stitch the binding in place over the machine-stitching line on the backside. Hand-miter the corners on the back as shown in Figure 20.

If you are making a quilt to be used on a bed, you may want to use double-fold, bias-grain bindings because the many threads that cross each other along the fold at the edge of the quilt make it a more durable binding.

Cut 2¼"-wide bias strips from a large square of fabric. Join the strips as illustrated in Figure 16 and press the seams open. Fold the beginning end of the bias strip ¼" from the raw edge and press. Fold the joined strips in half along the long side, wrong sides together, and press with no steam (Figure 21).

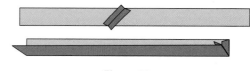

**Figure 21**
Fold and press strip in half.

Follow the same procedures as previously described for preparing the quilt top and sewing the binding to the quilt top. Treat the corners just as you treated them with straight-grain binding.

Since you are using bias-grain binding, you do have the option to just eliminate the corners if this option doesn't interfere with the patchwork in the quilt. Round the corners off by placing one of your dinner plates at the corner and rotary-cutting the gentle curve (Figure 22).

**Figure 22**
Round corners to eliminate
square-corner finishes.

As you approach the beginning of the binding strip, stop stitching and lay the end across the beginning so it will slip inside the fold. Cut the end at a 45-degree angle so the raw edges are contained inside the beginning of the strip (Figure 23). Resume stitching to the beginning. Bring the fold to the back of the quilt and hand-stitch as previously described.

**Figure 23**
End the binding strips as shown.

Overlapped corners are not quite as easy as rounded ones, but a bit easier than mitering. To make overlapped corners, sew binding strips to opposite sides of the quilt top. Stitch edges down to finish. Trim ends even.

Sew a strip to each remaining side, leaving 1½"–2" excess at each end. Turn quilt over and fold binding down even with previous finished edge as shown in Figure 24.

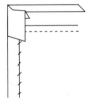

**Figure 24**
Fold end of binding even with
previous page.

Fold binding in toward quilt and stitch down as before, enclosing the previous bound edge in the seam as shown in Figure 25. It may be necessary to trim the folded-down section to reduce bulk.

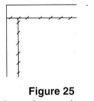

**Figure 25**
An overlapped corner is not quite as
neat as a mitered corner.

## Final Touches

If your quilt will be hung on the wall, a hanging sleeve is required. Other options include purchased plastic rings or fabric tabs. The best choice is a fabric sleeve, which will evenly distribute the weight of the quilt across the top edge, rather than at selected spots where tabs or rings are stitched, keep the quilt hanging straight and not damage the batting.

To make a sleeve, measure across the top of the finished quilt. Cut an 8"-wide piece of muslin equal to that length—you may need to seam several muslin strips together to make the required length.

Fold in ¼" on each end of the muslin strip and press. Fold again and stitch to hold. Fold the muslin strip lengthwise with right sides together. Sew along the long side to make a tube. Turn the tube right side out; press with seam at bottom or centered on the back.

Hand-stitch the tube along the top of the quilt and the bottom of the tube to the quilt back making sure the quilt lies flat. Stitches should not go through to the front of the quilt and don't need to be too close together as shown in Figure 26.

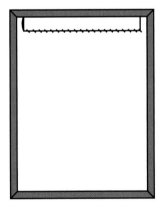

**Figure 26**
Sew a sleeve to the top back of the quilt.

Slip a wooden dowel or long curtain rod through the sleeve to hang.

When the quilt is finally complete, it should be signed and dated. Use a permanent pen on the back of the quilt. Other methods include cross-stitching your name and date on the front or back or making a permanent label which may be stitched to the back.